THE JEWISH GUIDE TO
MANIFESTING

THE JEWISH GUIDE TO MANIFESTING

BASED ON TORAH SOURCES AND WISDOM

RABBI YAAKOV COHEN

Mosaica Press, *with its team of acclaimed editors and designers, is attracting some of the most compelling thinkers and teachers in the Jewish community today. Our books are impacting and engaging readers from around the world.*

Copyright © 2024 by Mosaica Press

All rights reserved. No part of this book may be used or reproduced or transmitted in any form or by any means, electronic or mechanical, including photocopying, recording, or by any information storage and retrieval system, without written permission from the publisher.

ISBN: 978-1-961602-50-2

Published by Mosaica Press, Inc.
www.mosaicapress.com
info@mosaicapress.com

CHAPTERS 1–7

Special thanks to

DANIEL SARFATI

my beloved student

May you and your family be blessed with success, joy, and fulfillment.

CHAPTER 8

Special thanks to

KAENAN AND DAFNA HERTZ AND FAMILY

May Hashem continue to bless you with many years
of growth in Torah and mitzvos.

Rabbi Zev Leff

Rabbi of Moshav Matityahu
Rosh HaYeshiva—Yeshiva Gedola Matityahu

הרב זאב לף בס"ד

מרא דאתרא מושב מתתיהו
ראש הישיבה—ישיבה גדולה מתתיהו

D.N. Modiin 71917   Tel: 08-976-1138 'טל   Fax: 08-976-5326 'פקס   ד.נ. מודיעין 71917

Dear Friends,

I have read portions of the "Jewish Guide to Manifesting" by Rabbi Yaakov Cohen. The author presents the importance and power of thought as found in the wisdom of Torah sources. The physical world is but a manifestation of spiritual forces that emanate from Hashem, the ultimate source of everything. Hashem, the Creator and sustainer of all existence designated spiritual emanations that manifest His will in the world that we see and experience. Hence, proper thoughts can affect these spiritual forces and result in positive or G-d forbid negative effects in the world in general and in one's own personal life. The author discusses the various types of thoughts that one should utilize to manifest positive results according to various Torah sources.

I found the work interesting, informative and inspiring. I found the material to be representing true Torah concepts. I recommend this book for all those who desire to learn about the efficacy of positive thinking and who wish to enhance their spiritual and material lives and the world in general by putting these ideas into practice.

I commend the author for a fine presentation and pray that Hashem bless-him and his family with life and health and the wherewithal to continue to merit the community.

Sincerely,
With Torah blessings

Rabbi Zev Leff

TABLE OF CONTENTS

Acknowledgments xi
Prologue xiii
Introduction 1

CHAPTER ONE: Tending the Garden of the Mind 7
CHAPTER TWO: The Importance of Our Thoughts 25
CHAPTER THREE: Discovering and Shifting Patterns 42
CHAPTER FOUR: Expanding Our Measure 68
CHAPTER FIVE: The Torah—The Best and Only
    Kosher Thought Diet 84
CHAPTER SIX: Quantum Thinking 106
CHAPTER SEVEN: Focusing 122
CHAPTER EIGHT: Dynamic World Change 130

Epilogue 151
Appendix 152

ACKNOWLEDGMENTS

DEDICATED TO THE HOLY ONE, blessed be He, and His holy Shechinah.

Thank You, Hashem, for allowing this book to be born, as a mother gives birth to a child.

To my Rosh Yeshiva, Rabbi Mordechai Goldstein, *zt"l*, of the Diaspora Yeshiva, who brought me under the wings of the holy Shechinah and whose dedicated teaching inspired this work.

This book is also dedicated to my most beautiful and righteous wife, Devorah, and all my amazing children whom God has blessed me with: Michal, Yonatan, Tamar, Talia, Elisha, Shayna, and Shabtai.

To my wonderful parents, to whom no amount of gratitude can adequately be expressed: my father, Dr. Harvey Cohen, who has been my original inspiration from whom so much of the spirit and material in this book derives, and my mother, Daphne Neiman Cohen, for all of her continued support, for always believing in me, and instilling me with my strong Jewish identity.

To my holy father-in-law and mother-in-law, Rabbi Shabtai and Helen Teicher, for always supporting us. Rabbi Shabtai, *zt"l*, Kabbalist and author of the *Zohar* on *Saba D'Mishpatim*, dedicated years to teaching me the inner wisdom of the Kabbalah, while my mother-in-law is always there for our family.

To Rebbetzin Yeshara Gold, whose inspiration was the catalyst for me to continue this book.

Thanks to Rabbi Doron Kornbluth, who gave me the encouragement to go forward with publishing this work. Thanks as well to Rabbi Yaacov Haber, copublisher of Mosaica Press, and the entire team for their outstanding work.

PROLOGUE
A COSMIC OUTLOOK

WHAT IF THIS WORLD were like a cosmic field in which we were all making our own reality, to some degree? Here we are, in this strange world, saturated with limitations and obstacles. We are each actually a soul injected into a physical body. What really is going on above us is hidden from us, and we are here to discover that we have been creating the whole time. Yes, there is a Creator Who is overseeing everything. He makes the universe user-friendly for us to realize we are all creating our reality, and it all comes down to the thoughts that we think and what we believe. Of course, it's very hard for a limited mind to approach an unlimited mind. So, the Unlimited Creative Intelligence gave us the instruction manual, i.e., the Torah, to develop unlimited-style thinking.

In the end, if after all the work on thinking the right thoughts and working on creating those angels, we don't get the outcome that we wanted, can we say about ourselves, "We didn't think the right thoughts. We didn't believe it enough. We doubted it"? Can one say such a thing?

Read on to find out why.

INTRODUCTION
THE KOSHER THOUGHT DIET

I WRITE WITH great trepidation, knowing that whatever I include in this book, I must also strive to live by. May it be God's will that we all live by what is written here.

Much has been written on the concept of how thought becomes form—the idea that the thoughts we think become our reality. Most of the material that can be found today on this topic comes from secular books that repeat this idea over and over again. My goal is only to bring a few sources from Biblical and ancient Hebraic spiritual texts to give us deeper insight, clarity, and truth to this matter.

Once you understand the principles of thought, you will see them scattered everywhere in the holy books. All the books of our holy masters are in sync on this subject.

This idea—that thoughts create reality—is so powerful that, if taken seriously, we can understand how it can bring about change not only in our personal lives, but also in the general rectification of the world.

My mission became apparent after witnessing my father, who is a great teacher in this concept, suffer an inoperable brain tumor. In 1996, when he was diagnosed with the tumor, he was given between two weeks and two months to live. He decided not to undergo any treatments.[1] Even after my pleading with him to try herb tinctures

---

[1] May God protect us from all sickness. This was my father's own decision. Anyone in such a situation or similar, God forbid, should consult with their rabbi.

and diet plans, he urged me to support him on his position to "look only to God for peace of mind" and do nothing else. Despite the idea that God sends us vehicles for healing (akin to the parable of the person in the flood who allows a log, a boat, and a helicopter to pass him by, saying, "God will save me!" who subsequently dies and goes before God saying, "Why didn't You save me?" whereupon God replies, "I sent you a log, a boat, and a helicopter!"), and our obligation to take certain actionable measures, my father said, "If I take the tincture or diet plan and become healed, it will detract from my faith."

My wife and I relocated from Israel and took jobs in Los Angeles. We would bring him food and have him spend time with his grandchildren. Sometimes, he would just sit in his recliner meditating; other times, he would write. Sometimes, he was struck with a terrible migraine that forced him to retreat to his bedroom to lie down. Every ten minutes, one side of his body would suddenly shake. Yet, the year passed by, and dad was still around. His body wasn't trembling anymore. I recall walking around the same park that we had been in the year before, when we had discussed his plan of total faith. Now, he was telling me that after one of his friends had pushed him to go for tests, he had reluctantly gone—and the hospital had lost his X-rays. He said, "Forget it." Then the hospital called him back, saying they had found the X-rays and that there was not even a trace of a brain tumor.

There are obviously many ways to explain such a miraculous recovery. Personally, I was struck by the question of how true it is that our thoughts create our experiences and reality. Here my father, who for years had preached that "it's all in the mind," was put in the position of walking the walk. All the years I was in rabbinical school, I had been reading my father's books about the power of thought on circumstance (I was raised on the stuff!). Still, a yeshiva student is trained to seek the truth and not take everything he hears at face value. The Torah, being the blueprint of Creation, must contain the source and wisdom of everything.

After my father's experience, this issue seriously gnawed at my brain. I knew that God demands of us to proactively guard our lives and make efforts for our health and well-being. But to witness the pure faith that my father displayed made me question the whole "effort vs. total trust" thing. I started on a quest, asking every learned man whom I knew in an attempt to reconcile these seemingly disparate views. I knew some of the relevant texts, but I wanted to hear it from the mouth of the masters themselves.

This book is the result of my small survey of some of the rabbis in Jerusalem and some of my own research. I must give credit to my father, as many of the demonstrations and imagery in this book come from the teachings of my father.

AFTER RETURNING TO ISRAEL, I remember standing in the kitchen of Rabbi Shalom Gold's house in which Rabbi Avromel Brog was present. After relating what just happened with my father, Rabbi Brog immediately told us the following story of Rabbi Chaim Volozhin and the gold watch:

The Rav was sitting with his students one night in the study house discussing matters of faith and such topics. He said, "If you believe in something enough—anything!—you can get it."

"Anything?" one of the students retorted.

"How about a gold watch?" another student challenged. (Watches were not easy to come by in those days, let alone gold ones.)

The Rav answered, "Challenge accepted. And so shall we do."

The Rav then proceeded to engage his students in certain strategies of thought and faith. He continued working with them through different activities until late at night. On and on they continued—perhaps practicing prayer, affirmations, meditation, or dancing—when suddenly, at around two o'clock in the morning, a young man came bursting in.

"Rebbi, Rebbi," the stranger said. "I've been drafted into the Polish army; I'm on my way to report to them right now. I need you to do me a favor and hold this watch for me. I am the son of a wealthy man. My father's attempt to get me an exemption failed. I must go now, but I have no one to leave this watch with."

"Wait," the Rav answered. "How can I be responsible for such a valuable item? I don't know who you are or if I'll be ever able to find you."

"You know," answered the stranger. "Just keep the watch. Better that you have it than for someone else steal it from me."

With that, the young man walked out to report to the army, leaving the gold watch in the Rav's hand.

Of course, we are not after gold watches. The Rav was simply demonstrating the principle that if one believes and focuses his mind, he can achieve.

There are an overwhelming number of sources that support the idea that our thoughts create our circumstances. To go through all of them would take volumes. Instead, I chose to bring the most inspiring and relevant in this small book for the purpose of impact. I wrote the ideas very concisely, and each can be expounded upon greatly. My intention is simply to awaken the reader so that they can continue exploring and discovering in their life where these ideas can take them.

Exploring the source material on this subject compels us to at least take notice of the perceptions, thoughts, and attitudes we habitually utilize. It is our obligation to know the truth of this idea and how much it applies to us personally and globally. In truth, the entire Torah is a "thought diet." Although it is enough that, by engaging in Torah learning, one is fulfilling the will of the Creator, when one also understands that they are reprogramming their mind and developing a higher level of thinking, they can also elevate themselves and humanity. The only obstacles are their preconceived attitudes, perceptions, and limitations. Emptying themselves and seeing the Torah anew with "higher soul thinking glasses" will bring them to fulfillment and wholeness.

WHY IS THIS BOOK so important?

We have been taught, "Open for Me an opening the size of the point of a needle, and I will open for you celestial gates."[2]

As we will see in later chapters, God created the world in order for us to appreciate and have a relationship with Him, the Infinite Source. For this relationship, it is necessary for there to be what is called an "awakening from below" in order for there to be a bestowal from above.[3] The Almighty is telling us that we must make some effort, even if it is as tiny as the point of a needle.

Certainly, this tiny effort should be expressed in action, which is the greatest manifestation of effort. But all action begins in thought, and the right thoughts do indeed awaken and inspire to say or do the highest. This book is about focusing and enhancing our thoughts to motivate us toward our personal and global redemption.

WE FIRST LEARN the principle of an "awakening from below" from Adam in the Garden of Eden. The verse says, "And there was no foliage, for there was no man to work the ground." The eleventh-century commentators explain that even though God created the grasses and trees on the third day of Creation, they did not yet sprout from the

---

2 *Zohar, Vayikra* 95a. Rabbi Daniel Frisch comments that a small awakening from below awakens much from above. See also Rabbi Tzadok Hakohen, *Tzidkas Hatzaddik* #41.

3 See Rabbi Shlomo Elyashiv, *Leshem Shevo V'Achlamah*, part 2, which discusses why Moshe and Aharon first gathered all the elders of Israel to tell them of the redemption before going to Pharaoh. They needed to be awakened first for there to be a bestowal of Pharaoh letting the people go. The redemption would not have happened had they not been awakened.

ground. They needed rain, which makes everything grow, but God had not yet brought the rain because there was to no one to pray for it. There was no one to appreciate that rain brings life.

Thereupon, He created Man, who came to realize that rain was necessary for everything to sprout and grow. And so, Adam prayed for rain, which allowed him to appreciate the rain and its source. There has to be a vessel of appreciation: an awakening, an awareness of lacking, and then a fulfillment of that lacking. For our redemption, we must awaken and initiate our coming close to and connecting with the Infinite.

"Open for Me an opening the size of the point of a needle." What is this small point of the needle? I boldly say that it starts with our will, thoughts, and yearnings. The purpose of this book is to grasp that every thought is a creative force.

IMPORTANT NOTE: This book is meant to be a personal journey, and its ideas should not be imposed upon anyone else who may be on a different journey.

As you read this book, please take note of the phrases in gray boxes. These phrases are intended to help generate opportunities for us to create those forces that will open up a greater potential for us to experience.

Enjoy!

CHAPTER ONE
TENDING THE GARDEN OF THE MIND

THERE ARE MANY places in our holy writings that liken our minds and lives to a garden. The following are just a few places to give us a stage and setting.

IN THE IMAGE OF GOD

To set the stage, we must first realize with absolute certainty our creative power.

> *And God created man in His image. In the image of God, He created him.*
>
> Bereishis 1:27

What does it mean that we were created in the image and likeness of God?

Since we know that God has no image, what could that image be? "Image" refers to a conceptual mold or structure that the Creator designed to make man.[1] Of the many aspects of this conceptual mold are the will and thoughts, and also a structure to bring those thoughts

---

[1] See Rabbeinu Bachya, *Bereishis* 1:27, who explains that this refers to the ten *Sefiros* or ten Illuminations in which the Creator interacts with the Creation. See Rabbi Aryeh Kaplan, *Inner Space*, chap. 3.

down to expression. "Likeness of God" primarily means that we were made to have understanding and gain wisdom.[2] Both image and likeness are in the area of thinking, including the ability to be creative.

Just as God's expression begins from His will—a thought—and then proceeds to the manifestation of that thought,[3] so too does man follow this same process. First, he thinks a thought, and then he proceeds to express it. For example, man first gets an idea to build a house, then has detailed plans drawn up, and then works to bring those plans to full manifestation. The imagery used in Kabbalah for the first impulse of creativity is that of a seed, which subsequently becomes implanted in the mind. The mind is the fertile soil, always seeking to bring out whatever is planted within it. As we are aware, a seed only knows how to produce more of its own kind: A wheat kernel cannot sprout corn, and a peach pit cannot grow avocados. Similarly, our mind can only produce experiences based on the seeds planted within it. The mind is also likened to an oven. An oven doesn't care what you place inside it; it just bakes it. You can't expect to put dirt in an oven and produce a cake.

We must be aware that our minds are very much like fertile soil with seeds being planted within that are in a state of constant creating! The fact that our minds are operating all the time gives us the ability to actualize our dynamic, creative nature. At any time, we can willfully direct those thoughts. Certain "will thoughts" are seeds that need

---

[2] See *Rashi, Bereishis* 1:26, and *Seforno* ad loc. For another explanation, see also *Nefesh Hachaim* 1:3: "God empowered mankind to control and influence countless forces and worlds through his actions, words, and thoughts."

[3] The Kabbalistic meaning of the Tetragrammaton (*Yud-Kei-Vav-Kei*) is an expression going from will and thought to manifestation, or "thought-manifest" for short. The first letter, *yud*, is the first thought in seed form. It has no detailed plan or image of expression. The next letter, *hei*, is the detailed imagery or visualization in the mind. The next letter, *vav*, is the force that implements the mental plan, and the final letter, *hei*, is the actualization of the original letter *hei*—hence, the manifestation of thought.

to be planted, nurtured, and grown. A great place to exercise this awareness is the first law of the code of Jewish laws, namely, to wake up like a lion to serve the King of Kings—to awaken and utilize our creative process to proactively create our days and lives.

> "I am a powerful creative entity! I will utilize the creative nature God has given me to create my day!"

And from the ground God caused to grow every tree that was pleasing to the sight and good for food, with the Tree of Life in the middle of the garden and the Tree of Knowledge of Good and Evil.

Bereishis 2:9

Let's examine the commentary of the Chassidic Rebbe, Rabbi Tzadok Hakohen of Lublin:

- "The Garden of Eden sprouts from it all trees **pleasing to the sight**"—this represents the external, outer expression of a person's deeds.
- "**Good for food**"—this represents the inner aspect of a person, i.e., his thoughts and feelings. From the comparison between food and thought, it seems that thoughts are a higher form of energy intake.
- "**The Tree of Life**"—this represents the heart of a person (i.e., the will), as it is placed in the middle part of the body.
- "**And the Tree of Knowledge**"—this represents the mind that distinguishes between good and evil.[4]

---

4 Rabbi Tzadok Hakohen, *Kometz Haminchah* 2:26.

> *And God took the man and placed him in the Garden of Eden to work it and guard it.*
>
> Bereishis 2:16

There are several commentators who do not view the Garden of Eden as a literal garden but rather as a spiritual concept.[5] The verse says that God placed Adam there to "work and guard." What does this mean? Were there thieves roaming around that one needs to guard from? From here, we can infer that the verse is referring to a garden that has spiritual needs. Just like land needs to be worked, plowed, and seeded, so too, this garden of the soul needs planting and guarding. To "work" represents the good deeds, and to "guard" symbolizes refraining from negative actions. The *Zohar* specifically associates the verse with positive and negative commandments. A person's actions are therefore likened to tending a garden. Hence, your life is your garden.

> *When you besiege a city for many days to wage war upon it…you must not destroy its trees. You may eat of them, but you may not cut them down. For the trees of the field are a person…*
>
> Devarim 20:19

From this verse, we derive the prohibition against the needless destroying of items. This verse specifically refers to fruit trees—that we may partake of them but not cut them down. What is interesting is the reason given for the prohibition, which is that the Torah compares a person to a tree. The most common understanding is that the life of humankind is dependent on the food of the trees of the field. We are not to cut them down because they can benefit someone. The Talmud

---

[5] Rabbi Chaim ben Attar, *Ohr Hachaim*, *Bereishis* 2:15; *Zohar* 27a.

brings the deeper meaning as to why man is compared to a tree.[6] Fruit trees are likened to scholars and people of good influence, whom we may not cut down. Non-fruit-bearing trees are likened to people of bad influence, whom we are encouraged to stay away from. This idea is expressed by many other sources.[7] Just as trees start from seeds and have roots, branches, and fruit, so too, all these elements are contained within man. The fruits only produce seeds of their own kind.

> *For thus says God to the men of Judah and to Jerusalem, "Break up the untilled ground and do not sow among thorns."*
>
> Yirmiyahu 4:3

The prophet Yirmiyahu is not literally instructing the men to start farming. The wording is being used in a metaphorical sense, telling them about the need for them to correct their deeds. Just as the farmers dig up the soil in the summer to kill the roots of the thorn weeds, ensuring that they won't rise at the time of planting, so too, we must make an effort to better our deeds before we plant our seeds of holiness. The idea of uprooting the thorns in our hearts represents ridding ourselves of the bad character traits and negative images that grow on the "mounds" of the heart. We need to do this before we plant the seeds of charity and good deeds that will draw us close to God.

We see from this metaphor how the heart and soul are likened to a field. "Do not plant your seeds [i.e., your thoughts] in a place of negativity." Your thoughts—which are the roots of your character traits and deeds—are seeds. They will grow.

---

6   *Taanis* 7a.
7   *Zohar* 1:187a, 3:202a, 3:215a, 3:219a; *Tikkunei Zohar* 141b. Here is the source for the Kabbalistic custom to celebrate the new year for trees each year on the fifteenth day of the month of Shevat. It is celebrated with special rituals likened to the Passover Seder.

Our lives in this world are likened to a garden or field. Our good thoughts, words, and deeds are likened to removing stones, cutting out weeds, plowing, planting, watering, and pruning our personal garden, which we can call our "holy garden."[8] What is this holy garden about? It intimates that we are participating in a cosmic event that is likened to a garden or field—a cosmic garden that we, as creations, are involved in building—which is a means that enables the holy Infinite to express His Infiniteness.

How we tend to our "holy garden" will determine our destiny and our unique expression, our part in Creation, and our portion in the fulfillment of our destiny. How much and in what way the Infinite expresses itself depends on how well we tend to this garden. Our Creator is the "Master Gardener," but we must do our part. The beginning of our work in the "garden" starts in the mind. We need to understand that when we accept and integrate thoughts and beliefs, it is like we are planting the seeds; the dynamic and fertile ground of our consciousness will grow whatever thought or belief we put into it. So, let us choose our seeds wisely.

CHOOSING YOUR SEEDS

The question is, which seeds should be implanted in our minds? We need to determine if they are good seeds or if they will not allow us to express our unique potential in life. If we can adopt and integrate the higher style of thinking that we will explain in later chapters, it will surely bring forth a higher experience—an experience of greater joy, trust, security, and fulfillment. We need to develop the ability to become aware of our thoughts.

Let us examine a key source that exposes the power of our thoughts.

---

8   Arizal, *Otzros Chaim, Shaar Nikudim*, chap. 6.

Angels from Thoughts

Our Sages share with us a life-changing principle: "The way in which a person wants to go, they lead him."[9]

The question is, who are the "they" that our Sages are talking about?

If this principle means that God leads a person in the way he wants to go, the Hebrew should have been written in the singular form: "In the way in which a person wants to go, He [i.e., God] leads him." But the Hebrew is in the plural form. So, the question remains, who are the "they" to whom the Sages are referring?

The answer is that **with every thought, word, and action a person thinks, says, or does, an angel is created.**[10]

However, whether the angel created is good or bad depends on the particular thought, word, or deed. This idea is simple yet astounding: Every thought creates an angel!

Additionally, the angel that is created as a result of a person's thought, word, or action enables the materialization of that thought, word, or action. In other words, we ourselves produce the force that will allow our thoughts to be manifested in the physical world. Our thoughts create angels, which in turn cause those thoughts to become reality.

This idea has significant implications, and it raises many questions. What exactly is an angel created by our thoughts? Does it literally mean every thought creates an angel? Is each angel the same? What about the angels we created in the past? Can anything be done about negative angels? If we change our thinking, can we change our angels? What would the result be?

Let's begin to answer these questions by understanding an important point: Not all thoughts are created equal. Some people generate

---

9 *Makkos* 10b.
10 Rabbi Shmuel Eliezer Edeles (1555–1631), known as the *Maharsha*. For a whole translation, see Appendix.

thoughts from the most powerful beliefs and convictions, while others have endless thoughts that sputter things out without any direction. Someone once explained it to me through an analogy of television newscasts. While there is a man announcing or analyzing a main news point, at the same time, there is something like a ticker tape with small news blurbs constantly moving on the bottom of the screen. Generally, the words racing by on the bottom don't have as much impact as the man talking.

The same thing occurs with our thoughts: There are heavier ones and weaker ones. Every thought is involved in creating angels, but some are more powerful. Indeed, we are taught that we are not responsible for the thoughts that just pop into our head—only for what we choose to do with those thoughts.

What Do We Mean Here by the Word "Angel"?

How do we understand the word "angel" according to the Torah? The *Rambam* defines an angel as an incorporeal, spiritual being with no shape or form that is capable of imparting information or prophetic messages to people.[11] The word "angel" may conjure up for some people images of a half-naked winged baby flying through the air, or a female-like figure in a flowing white gossamer gown, crowned with a glowing halo. Yet, there are many people who wouldn't even venture a guess as to what an angel looks like. How does this idea of an angel blend with what we are discussing here?

The answer is that angels are energies.

Let's look a little closer at this concept. We can all agree that different thoughts bring about different feelings. Maybe, the thought of your child or grandchild warms your heart with happiness, thinking about filling out your tax return brings about feelings of anxiety and dread,

---

11   *Rambam, Yesodei HaTorah* 2:3.

and anticipating your upcoming vacation in the Bahamas lifts your mood. Let's call these feelings "feeling tones." Specific thoughts elevate and inspire you, making you feel charged, while other thoughts make you feel depressed and bring you down.

Simply put, thoughts create a vibrational force—an energy that pulls you to carry out that thought and propel you to your destiny. This is the principle of resonance, and it can be illustrated by using tuning forks. We can take what we call an "A" tuning fork, and when we strike it, an "A" sound is produced. When we bring another motionless "A" tuning fork close to the vibrating one, what happens? The "A" vibration passes onto the other tuning fork, which then starts to emit its sound.[12]

Now, when we touch it with an "E" note, what happens? It stops. Although there are a lot of conclusions that one can draw from this phenomenon, the point I want to draw out here is that an "A" only knows how to connect with the same sound—another "A."

In the same way, our thoughts produce vibrations. And the thoughts we think, which produce those vibrations, only know how to find harmony with experiences in the same tone. Or like we said above, a wheat kernel only knows how to produce wheat; a corn kernel only knows how to bring forth corn. Wheat can't make corn, and corn cannot become wheat.

What does that tell us? The importance of becoming aware of our thoughts and being careful of the thoughts we think, because good thoughts produce positive angels—which we can also call a positive force or energy—while "bad" thoughts bring about a negative, destructive angel, which we can term a negative force.

---

12   This is also brought in the *Malbim*'s explanation of the Tabernacle that the Israelites built in the wilderness; see *Parashas Terumah*. If there are two instruments in a room, one in one corner and one in the other, and one of them is big and one of them is small, and I strike the chord on the bigger one, the same chord on the smaller instrument will resonate.

WEAKER VS. STRONGER ANGELS

We have explained that not all angels are equal; some are stronger, and some are weaker. The determining factors that make angels more or less powerful are based on two things: quantity and quality. It is estimated that a person thinks anywhere between 6,200 to 60,000 thoughts a day.[13] If we take the number 60,000, imagine if half of those thoughts are thought in one direction (for example, "I want such and such"), and the other half are focused on something else entirely. This would result in massive confusion. It's like an airplane with one engine facing one direction while the other engine faces a different direction. That aircraft isn't going to get anywhere—except maybe around in circles. This also answers the complaint that I so often hear, "Rabbi, why is my life going nowhere?"

There is the frequency with which thoughts recur in our psyche, and there is also the degree to which we believe in them. The extent to which our thoughts resonate with us determines the power of the angel created. The determining factor is the **conviction of the idea**.[14] This also illustrates the concept of "to the degree of the awakening from below will be the bestowal from above."[15]

---

13 For example, see research by Dr. J. Poppenk in *Nature Communications*, https://www.exploringtheproblemspace.com/new-blog/2017/1/1/counting-thoughts-part-i. Over twenty-four hours, one thought per second would yield 86,400 thoughts. If "thoughts" are restricted to sixteen waking hours, the number would be 57,600. But we're almost certainly thinking while we're dreaming (approximately two hours every night), so that would be 64,800 seconds, resulting in an average of one thought every 0.9257 seconds.

14 Imagine, for example, what the recitation of the *Shema* can do.

15 See *Leshem Shevo V'Achlamah, Sefer Hade'ah*, for why Moshe had to go to the Children of Israel before going to Pharaoh. Why did he say, "If the Children of Israel will not listen to me, how could Pharaoh?" Why should one relate to the other? The rule is that in order for there to be a bestowal from above, there must be a corresponding awakening from below. Thus, Moshe said, "If the Children of Israel don't believe in me to create this awakening from below that we need, how will Pharaoh listen to me to send them out?" Meaning, the

When we believe in something with great conviction, we are, in essence, striking a chord in our body, thereby manifesting a feeling. Thoughts create feeling tones. The feeling tones are resonances that only know how to affect or be affected by something of the same energy. Hence, the degree of one's conviction determines the power of the angel that is created. This explains, for example, why affirmations don't always work. You need to believe in them, and they must resonate with you because they will easily be destroyed by doubt.[16] In order to believe affirmations, they have to make total logical sense to you.

> *Where do thoughts come from?*
> *Thought is the essence of the man.*
> *Wisdom is the essence of thought.*
> Rabbi Tzadok Hakohen[17]

Have you ever wondered where thoughts come from? The mind is constantly thinking, yet we can grab the reins and refocus our thoughts whenever we choose to. The mind can wander unwittingly into the realms of fantasy and then, in a split second, shift to an important task. The mystics explain that there is a "place" known as the *mocha setima*—the hidden thought reservoir (or "will") that no one can touch.[18] It is in a dimension beyond which the "hidden thought" clothes itself in layers upon layers until it reaches the conscious mind. Our

---

bestowal from Pharaoh from "above." This is the concept of building the vessel for the light; the awakening from below builds the vessel for God to bestow the light within it.

16 The numerical value of the word for "doubt" (*safek*) is the same as the nation of Amalek, the nemesis of Israel.
17 Rabbi Tzadok Hakohen, *Machsheves Charutz*, beginning.
18 *Tikkunei Zohar*, end of *Tikkun* 19–41b, speaks about how Adam's sin caused levels of his soul to leave him, which is an element of death.

thoughts therefore emanate from a sublime, hidden dimension, which compose the higher elements of our soul.[19] The Baal Shem Tov teaches that **the soul dresses in the "will," and the "will" dresses in the thoughts. Our beliefs, will, and thoughts are therefore garments of the soul.**

We are referring here to lofty, high-level thoughts representing true wisdom—the thoughts that act as vessels or garments for our souls to help attain their ultimate self-expression.

Then there are thoughts that emanate from the body, which we generally call the place of the lower soul. The lower soul is the basic life force rooted in the body. It is very attached to the materialistic forces and has its own agenda, which hardly ever coincides with the agenda of the higher soul. The reason for its different agenda is that it is under the strong influence of the evil inclination, an angelic force given to us from birth.

Our main challenge in life is to align these two agendas (see below, chapter five). This is the battle between the good inclination and the bad inclination. Since thoughts are the garments of the soul, changing our thoughts will affect our "will," and in turn, our soul. But, as will be explained later, we must believe in those thoughts with conviction.

> *Better is a poor wise child than an old*
> *foolish king who no longer has the sense*
> *to heed warnings.*
> Koheles 4:13

---

19 See Arizal, *Eitz Chaim, shaar atik,* chap. 1, who mentions the *"mocha stima"* in the higher realms. See Rabbi Avraham Tzvi Kluger, *Divrei Chachamin B'Nachas,* vol. 2, 298.

King Solomon refers to the evil inclination as the "old foolish king," and the good inclination as the "poor wise child." The evil inclination enters a person at birth. It sets up its kingdom by establishing a network of perceptions, thoughts, and habits. Depending on a number of factors, it wires into the body a basic operating system. It uses the lower soul's inclinations to instill and maintain bad character traits. These are based on the four elements we have in the world: earth, wind, fire, and water. Earth draws a person to traits of sadness and depression, wind to instability and excessive speech, fire to anger, and water to chasing desires. The evil inclination pursues instant gratification in the physical world. It is referred to as "old" since it exists from the moment a person is born. It is referred to as a "king" because it dominates and goes unchecked. And it is referred to as "foolish" because it doesn't see the whole picture. Self-gratification in the here and now are its basic goals and tendencies, and it usurps the lower soul's energy to fulfill those desires.

The good inclination is referred to as the "poor wise child." We are taught that it does not enter a person until the age of twelve for a girl or thirteen for a boy. The good inclination is known in mysticism as the "mature intellect." In Hebrew, this is *"daas,"* the ability to know and discern.[20] The good inclination is referred to as "poor" because it has no pleasure to offer now; it only offers the idea of working now and receiving the reward later. It is referred to as "wise" because it perceives that if a person puts in the effort, he can acquire bliss in the World to Come. It is referred to as a "child" because it only arrives on the scene

---

20 *Zohar, Parashas Mishpatim* 98a; Arizal, *Eitz Chaim* 50:3, who uses the Kabbalistic terminology of *gevuros*, "powers of constriction," and *chassadim*, "forces of love" or expanded consciousness. Since the sin of Adam in the Garden of Eden, the powers of constricted consciousness enter the mind and psyche of a person first and exert their influence, which goes unchecked until the age of thirteen when the *chassadim*—or mature, loving forces of intellect—come in and begin the process of rectifying the original, unchecked powers.

from age twelve or thirteen, respectively. The holy *Zohar* explicitly refers to the good inclination and the evil inclination as angels.[21]

The goal of the "poor wise child" is to come and convince the "old foolish king"—along with its captive lower soul—to join forces as one to perform the will of the Creator.

THE WILL

The "will" is the point of meeting between the soul and the body.[22] Ultimately, it is the will that decides our direction in life: whether we follow the thoughts and voice of the lower soul or the higher soul. Neither soul has an independent will until it enters the body and becomes a novel creation called a "bodified soul." The will of the higher soul is to make the body a dwelling place for the Divine Presence, and this is intrinsically what the body desires too. There is, however, interference from the evil inclination, which seeks to dominate the body and the lower soul.

"In the way in which a person wants to go" refers to the will. The will is the factor that sets this process in motion, creating powerful angels. Indeed, the idea is to rectify the will, because from the will, proper thoughts can flow. It is the will that exists in every creation that gives birth to needs that reflect that original will. Those needs in turn give birth to thoughts and to intellectual considerations that work toward the original fulfillment of that will. For example, if a person's will to receive is limited only to animalistic lusts, their needs, thoughts, and even intellectual faculties will be subjugated to the purpose of fulfilling their animal needs. If another person's will is focused on honor or recognition, his intellectual faculties will be subjugated to that end.[23]

---

21 *Zohar Chadash, Acharei Mos* 57b–58a.
22 *Tikkunei Zohar*, end of *Tikkun* 19–41b.
23 See Rabbi Yehudah Leib Ashlag, known as the *Sulam*, in his introduction to *Zohar*, par. 21. Much of his writing explains that there are two types of will: the will to receive and the

The trick, which will be discussed later (in chapter five), is the unifying and magnifying of the will that becomes the ultimate, creative force.

An important principle to understand about the will is that while we might have many competing wills within ourselves—for example, the will to lose weight and the will to eat ice cream, among others—only one will can be dominant at a given time.

When this was explained to me, I was told to picture a funnel-like structure through which many wills are poised to pass through in order to fall into the "will chamber" or "will slot." But only one dominant will at a time may enter the focus area driving for that will's expression.

In general, the will can only stem from one of two categories: body (i.e., the evil inclination) or soul. The will of the body could be likened to "the Tree of Knowledge of Good and Evil," while the will of the soul could be likened to the "Tree of Life." I view these two trees in the center of the Garden of Eden as representing a state of confusion or doubt versus a state of clarity and certainty. The state of confusion can give rise to very strong and determined thoughts and wills of evil.

A person can become absolutely convinced that an evil act is essentially noble. Let's take the example of a person who must have his leg amputated because of gangrene, the result of many years of chain-smoking. Having urged him to quit smoking for years, his doctors believed that the necessity of amputation due to the irreparable damage would be a sufficient deterrent against further smoking. Yet, a year later, the same man was wheeled in to have his second leg amputated because he was still unable to quit smoking. The dominant will was screaming loudly from the body to continue smoking and refused to acknowledge any other will attempting to stop it. The will

---

will to bestow. The will to receive is essentially the fabric of all Creation, while the will to bestow is associated with the more spiritual, God-like attributes.

to listen to the doctors and quit smoking was hanging in the wings, weak and puny.[24]

Ask yourself: What is in your single "will slot"? Or to put it more directly, what do you want?

Spend a minute now and get some clarity. Usually, the body tends to take charge, pushing you to finish that ice cream in the freezer or the last piece of cake in the fridge. These are safe examples in which one would not get harmed in the *process* of choosing between the wills. The body-will tends to be very alacritous, pushy, and loud, and this is due to the effects of the Tree of Knowledge of Good and Evil, which brings about the sweet, rancid taste of confusion. **In reality, we have to proactively recapture our "will slot."** We must be consciously aware of this and never give up. The goal is to keep reclaiming our will slot joyously. If we are not yet able to focus consciously, we need not worry; after time and training, and learning to use the tools in this book and similar books, the good stuff will naturally move in.

> *Change your thoughts and you affect your will; affect your will and tap into your soul.*

DEALING WITH THE ANGELS OF THE PAST

The Name of the Most Powerful Angel

What happens when we say words like "I can't," "It's impossible," or "It's too hard"?

According to what we have been saying, if we catch ourselves thinking or speaking like this, we can create a force that will turn to us with a stop sign in its hand saying, "Sorry buddy, but you're not going

---

24 Rabbi Akiva Tatz, from a recorded class on the subject of free will.

here!" So, now there appears to be a barrier. And who is creating that barrier? You! Hence, we say, "A man's folly subverts his way, and his heart rages against God."[25]

One who continues thinking such thoughts each day is actually involved in creating and enhancing that barrier. Consider now that those 60,000 angel energies per day are actually forming the barrier between ourselves and our dreams. And we've been doing it for years, amounting to over 21.6 million angels per year! How can we go against and overcome this? Thank God, there is one angel that is the most powerful angel and can tear down any wall or barrier, and the name of that angel is… "Easy."

That's right. Because if you say the word "hard," what are you creating? You're creating a reality of hardness or difficulty. If you say "can't," you are creating the reality of "can't."

The solution to your challenge might not manifest itself as soon as you use this angel's name, but consider this: For God, nothing is hard (except man's foolishness and limited thinking). But for the Creator, everything is easy; to say otherwise would be heresy. So, when we are confronted with our challenge and say the word "easy" with conviction, we allow ourselves to be open to the solutions that normally would be closed off to our awareness.

> *The person was created to have dominion over the angels.*[26]

Which angels? Some commentaries say these include the cosmic angels such as Michael, Gavriel, and the like. Some say these refer to our evil inclination. Certainly, it includes an angel that seeks to challenge us every day into reinforcing bad habits, character traits, and worse. Even with the angels of the cosmic realm and the evil inclination,

---

25 *Mishlei* 19:3.
26 Rabbi Nachman of Breslov, *Likutei Moharan* 2:1.

there are also the angels of our thoughts. Before overpowering the evil inclination, which is so close to us, we must first achieve dominion over our thoughts, which become angels. We must make them strong and powerful, and send them before us to actualize whatever it is we made them for.

We must consciously commit to becoming a connoisseur of thoughts. Just like we would use our power of discernment to select which foods to eat—"only the best coffee" or "only the best chocolate"—so too, we must make a conscious decision to only allow the best thoughts to permeate our being. Truly, there is no better thought diet than our holy Torah, which was given to us by the Unlimited Oneness.

EXERCISE

Say to yourself:

- "I will try to be aware of the thoughts I think today."
- "I will try to catch myself whenever I think or say 'can't,' 'impossible,' or 'hard.'"
- "I will mentally decide to utilize my belief system and say the word 'easy' with belief and conviction because, for God, 'hard' just doesn't make sense. I will try to greet any challenge with "easy."

CHAPTER TWO
THE IMPORTANCE OF OUR THOUGHTS

IT WAS AN UNUSUALLY freezing winter in the town of Medzhybizh (pronounced Med-ji-bouge). As usual, the men of the town gathered in the synagogue for the morning prayers with their holy *rebbi*, the Baal Shem Tov. While the prayer service continued with the Baal Shem Tov leading the services, two men in the back of the synagogue saw through the window a wagon laden with firewood pulling up in the town square. Pre-cut wood was not easy to come by that winter, and everyone needed some to heat up their homes. The two men, who were now facing a dilemma, looked at each other. They were about to reach the holiest of moments in the service, when all the congregants respond together for the *Kedushah* prayer, where we praise God like the angels do, and which can only be said in a quorum of ten men. They thought to themselves: *We need wood! Do we leave and buy the wood and miss the prayer? Or do we bear with it, remain, and take the chance that there might be wood after the crowd outside has finished scouring the wagon? What to do?* One of the men went out and bought wood for his freezing cold dwelling, while the other obstinately stayed to say the holy prayer with his *rebbi*.

After the prayer service was over, the two men decided to ask their *rebbi* who had been in the right: the person who left or the person who stayed?

The Baal Shem Tov replied that the person who left to go outside and buy the wood was wishing that he hadn't had to leave the synagogue at such a special time. So, his mind was still in the synagogue, even though his body was outside—and wherever your thoughts are, that's where you are. As for the person inside the synagogue, his mind was outside buying the wood, even though his body was inside—because wherever your thoughts are, that's where you are.

> *Wherever your thoughts are,*
> *that is where you are.*
> Baal Shem Tov

This profound idiom smacks us right in the face. Profound, but what does it mean?

My body sits in the café or bookstore, and my thoughts are elsewhere—so you tell me that's where I am? How can that be? I'm experiencing my body in a crowded airport terminal, but my thoughts are of sitting on the beach, so that means that I'm not at the airport? If that were the case, vacations would be a lot easier and cheaper.

OUR SOULS ARE OUR ESSENCE

"Our essence is our soul, and our bodies are merely a garment encasing the lowest part of our soul."[1] Just as the shoe encases the lowest part of our bodies, so too, our bodies encase the lowest part of our souls.[2] This

---

1   See Rabbi Chaim Vital, *Shaarei Kedushah*, who quotes the verse, "On the flesh of a person you shall not pour" (*Shemos* 30:32), and learns that the words "on the flesh" are contrasted to "of a person" to mean that "the flesh" is one thing, i.e., the garment, and the "person" is the essence, i.e., the soul. See also Rabbi Itamar Shwartz, *Bilvavi Mishkan Evneh*, "Getting to Know Yourself," where the major theme of the book is this topic.

2   The *Zohar* and the Arizal state that we have five levels of soul. These are, from lowest to

is one of the reasons why we don't wear leather shoes on Yom Kippur. The symbolism of removing our shoes corresponds to the shedding of our bodily influence. It's the day of "all soul," and we need to be reminded of this idea and actually live it for at least one day a year. We should carry the concept of that "day of shedding" with us for the rest of the year. Our essence is our soul, not our body.

Let us combine this idea with another concept from the holy Baal Shem Tov, which teaches the following:

> Our thoughts are the most sublime garments for our souls.

With this in mind, we can understand that while our body might be sitting in the synagogue or at home, if our thoughts are elsewhere, that is where our non-localized soul is.

Our mind is our least-limited faculty. We can imagine ourselves sitting on a beach on the most beautiful sunny shore, and a second later, we can see ourselves standing under a barrage of thunder and lightning at the foot of Mount Sinai, about to experience the ultimate connection with the Unlimited Creative Intelligence. We can even project ourselves into the future, where our life has been shown to us as an unfolded open letter and we see all the dark areas of our life and how they were perfectly orchestrated for our benefit. The mind has the ability to traverse time, space, and consciousness. We are often asked questions such as "What do you want to be?" or "Who do you want to be?" Now we have new questions we can ask at any given moment: "Where do you want to be?" or "Where are you in the world?"[3]

---

highest: (1) *nefesh*—resting, (2) *ruach*—wind, (3) *neshamah*—breath, (4) *chayah*—life, and (5) *yechidah*—uniqueness.

3   See Rabbi Nachman of Breslov's story of *The Lost Princess*. Both times when the viceroy

We must catch ourselves whenever our thoughts begin to wander, stopping and asking ourselves, "Is this a good place? Is this where I really want to be?" Many times, the force of habit or otherwise can lead our soul to dreadful places. When we think destructive thoughts or dwell on negativity, it is as if we are dragging our soul—our essence—to the gutter or the garbage heap. We are in places of spiritual stench. The truth, however, is that our higher souls actually exist in the most incredible dimensions, right here and now, basking in connection to the Infinite.[4] And to get there is just a thought away. Our job is to master our thoughts and choose where we will be.

OUR THOUGHTS IN SPACE, TIME, AND CONSCIOUSNESS

Our holy books teach that our reality is divided into space, time, and consciousness.[5] Our essence can be driven to one or more of these three zones. We can see that to practice always being present offers the greatest opportunity to do a mitzvah, our highest expression of our true self. We find so many times in the day that our thoughts are in places where our body is not. The main way to do this is to always fill in the blank of one of these two statements: "Here and now, I am aware of _____," and "Here and now, I feel _____." Answering these questions will, God willing, bring us back to the present.

- **Space**—We must stop and catch ourselves when our minds lead us to another physical place on the planet, especially if we are talking with another person and, all the more so, in

---

of the king awakens from his sleep, he queries, "Where am I in the world?" This was also God's question to Adam in the Garden of Eden after the sin: "Where are you?"

4   See *Nefesh Hachaim* 1:15, citing *Sanhedrin* 91a. See Rabbi Aryeh Kaplan, *Inner Space*, p. 17. See also Rabbi Avraham Yitzchak Kook, *Olas Reiyah* 1:11: "Our souls are in perpetual prayer, always connected to our Infinite Source, Whom we call God. When we pray, we bring all the other aspects of ourselves and hook them into that zone."

5   *Sefer Yetzirah* 1:1.

communication with our Creator. Do we find ourselves mentally at our place of work or at a baseball game during our silent prayer? Your physical body might be standing in prayer, but if your mind is at the shopping mall, then that is where you truly are. So, when you're standing before the Creator, are you really with Him at that time?

- **Time**—Are your thoughts on future worries or past upsets? Nothing more needs to be said here. The future is not our world, and the past is gone.[6]
- **Consciousness**—Consciousness refers to intention for good or evil.[7] Things can be tricky here because of the effects of the Tree of Knowledge of Good and Evil, which contribute to the great degree of confusion in which many of us find ourselves. Some things can be easily deemed good and some easily evil, and then there is the gray area. Studying the laws of conduct is known to repair the effect of the Tree of Knowledge of Good and Evil. When we are able to bring clarity to every one of our actions and behave morally, we thus separate the good from the evil. Here, our intentions as well as our knowledge play a key role. Are we really doing something for the sake of others or the world, or are we doing it for our egotistical self?

---

6 However, there is the Torah of Rabbi Nachman that says one must always be careful and preserve memory, and the way to do that is to always keep in mind the future world. This is the *quantum thought* discussed later on in chapter seven. The lost princess we are looking for is no longer in the dark castle, but, rather, can only be found on the golden mountain and the pearl castle.

7 These are the *Sefiros*/Dimensions of *Kesser*, crown, the highest of the ten *Sefiros*, and *Malchus*, kingship, the lower of the ten, as is brought in *Sefer Yetzirah*. It must be noted, however, that *Malchus* herself is not evil, God forbid, but, rather, because of her position as the ultimate receiver, she is *in the direction* of evil. See Rabbi Yehudah Leib Ashlag, *Sulam*, introduction to *Zohar*, p. 15, who explains two types of will to receive: one to receive on condition to bestow, and the other to receive for itself alone.

Some Examples of Thoughts in Space, Time, and Consciousness

The teachings of the Baal Shem Tov were written down by his many students. One of those students was Rabbi Yaakov Yosef of Polonye. The following passage is an example that includes all three dimensions and fits with the theme of this book. He writes:

> It is taught in the Talmud that each one of the 613 mitzvos corresponds to one of the limbs of the body.[8] If so, how is it that one mitzvah that a person does with **one of the limbs of his body results in creating an angel that has all 613 limbs?** If you did a mitzvah with a leg, it should just be a leg angel?
>
> The answer is that when a person does a mitzvah with complete faith that through that particular mitzvah he merits to attach to the Infinite Oneness, may He be blessed, he becomes connected to God, as the verse says, "And to Him, you will attach." To attach oneself to God is the prime directive of the entire Torah. Attachment or connectedness is the fruit of the tree of the Torah, its ultimate expression. If so, then when he is attached, he binds his thoughts to the Infinite One, so consequently, all 248 limbs and 365 sinew nerves are dragged along, as I heard from my teacher the Baal Shem Tov: Wherever a person's thoughts are, that is where he is completely. (So, for example, this person who did the act of charity with only his right hand: since his thoughts were attached above, so his whole body was attached along with the hand that did the actual act.)

---

[8] The 248 positive commandments correspond to the 248 limbs, and the 365 negative commandments correspond to the 365 sinews. *Zohar, Vayishlach* 170b.

> This is why the prophet Chavakuk stood the Torah's fulfillment for the later generations on one thing. He says, "The righteous man lives b'emunaso." This word is classically translated as "faith," but according to Rabbi Lazer Brody, emunah means "one's connection to Hakadosh Baruch Hu." Hence Chavakuk's assertion is that the tzaddik will live through his connection to Hashem. When one is attached to God, one is beyond time, space, and limitation.

Space in Thought

Another example is from Yaakov our forefather regarding the dream of the ladder.[9] The angels who were going up were the angels of the Land of Israel, and the angels coming down were the angels outside of Israel. The place where he was sleeping was the location of the Temple Mount. The question is that since Yaakov hadn't actually left Israel yet, why should these angels be going up and those coming down? The answer is that since Yaakov's mind was already outside of Israel, so too was he considered outside.

Consciousness in Thought

Elisha the Prophet offers a bold example regarding consciousness in thought. The mind of Elisha was always in the upper worlds. That affected his lower world to such a degree that there was never a fly seen at his table. His vibrational frequency was so high that flies could not exist in any plane of his existence and experience. When a person's mind is in a very high and holy place, God does not show that person unholy things.

What is the meaning of "to have our minds on the upper worlds"? Although there are many explanations that can be very esoteric, we are

---

9   As explained by the *Shem MiShmuel, Parashas Vayeitzei*.

going to attempt a simple and basic one using a well-known parable. There once was a man who, after he had passed away and was being led by an angel to his place in Gan Eden, made a simple request to first see what Gehinnom[10] was like. The angel gladly honored his request, "pushed the elevator button to go downward," so to speak, whereupon the doors to Gehinnom opened. The man saw huge tables laden with the most lavish delicacies and the most amazing aroma permeating the air. Sitting around the tables were scores of hungry people screaming to eat, yet they were unable to feed themselves because their arms had been placed in immobilizing splints that forced their arms to jet out to their sides. Horrified, the man turns to the angel and says, "I've seen enough, thank you."

Brought back into the elevator, the angel then brings the man to Gan Eden. Lo and behold, he again sees huge tables with all the same lavish food and aromas, everybody there similarly sitting around the table, and their arms also stuck in the very same position as the tortured souls he'd seen in Gehinnom! Unlike in Gehinnom, however, where people were only thinking about themselves, in Gan Eden the positioning of the arms actually helped! Here, in Gan Eden, all the people fed each other, and their extended arms made it easier for them to do that!

What we see is that the primary difference between Gan Eden and Gehinnom is the idea of egotistic self-absorption: Are people focused only on themselves and stuffing their face, or are they focused on others? The parable is simplified. There are many levels to selfishness, and there are just as many to thinking of others—to the degree we become more Godlike, as God only desires the benefit of others. He doesn't need anything and neither does He need to receive anything. He is only interested in giving as the Torah defines it. The degree

---

10   Loosely translated as "Purgatory."

man equates himself with that form will be that person's degree of attachment to God and the upper realms. The holy man's mind is always working to benefit mankind; to advance his generation and humanity as a whole; to be in the realm of *atzilus*,[11] the highest of the spiritual realms in Jewish tradition; to be at the root connection to the holy Shechinah, the Divine Presence.

Being Present

The biggest challenge of the current generation is staying present. Besides for their dwelling on mistakes of the past or their worries about the future, most people's minds are distracted by technology and other diversions. For many, their situation in the present is not that appealing, and they find themselves aching to get out of their present situation, whether it be a job, relationship, or living space. So, of course, their thoughts and souls will be elsewhere.

Sometimes we find ourselves in a situation where someone is pouring out their heart to us, telling us their life's problems and challenges. The person is sharing deep issues, and we might feel an urge to be somewhere, anywhere else. We are not present with the person. Obviously, according to the rules of specific Divine Providence, we are meant to be there with the person before us. If our minds wander to other places, then that is where our soul is. How could we do such a thing? Perhaps, if our soul would also be there, we would rejoice that we are fulfilling our life's purpose.[12]

The holy masters were actually living these moments as if they were before the Shechinah. Using this perception was actually the healing

---

[11] Literally the dimension of Nearness, which is classically called Emanation.

[12] I think the key is really *emunah*—to believe that God wants us to be in that situation with that challenge, whatever it might be. We need to learn to accept the situations in which we find ourselves with love, and from there, we thank God for the opportunity, yearning and praying for a higher experience.

technique of the Baal Shem Tov. When he would visit the sick or people would visit him with problems, along with that person's suffering, he would know and feel that what he is experiencing down here in the physical realm is really a reflection of what is taking place with the Shechinah in the higher spiritual realms, since everything down here is a reflection of what is in Heaven. He would pray on behalf of the Shechinah that the Infinite would bring relief or fill the void. Then, the healing would reverberate to a manifestation below with the person before him, and the person would be healed or his suffering would be lightened.

The following is a collection of treasures I have found that are impactful regarding the power of thought.

FIRST THOUGHT OF THE DAY, WEEK, OR YEAR

In the beginning of *Parashas Ki Savo*, Hashem commands us to take the first fruits and bring them to the Kohen as a thanksgiving offering to God. Why did the Torah command us to offer the first of our produce and not the best of it? The first of the produce may not be the best of the crop! What is so important about the first?

In *Baal Shem Tov on the Torah*, Rabbi Shimon Menachem Mendel Govartow explains that the importance of the "first" is that it is the root and foundation of all that follows. For example, the foundation of a building must be totally and completely perfect. A small crack in the foundation endangers the entire building, whereas that same crack would not be as significant if it would be on the fourth floor. Similarly, if we want something to be holy, its beginning must be holy and pure. We must recognize first that all our success comes from the Creator; there must be acknowledgment of the Infinite Source. Therefore, we dedicate all "firsts" to God to firmly establish the foundation and root of all that follows. So, along with first fruits, there are also, for example, the mitzvos of giving to the Kohen the firstborn male of all kosher animals, as well as redeeming from the Kohen the male firstborns of humans.

The Baal Shem Tov says that whatever your first thought is on any particular day stays with you, setting the pace for the rest of the day! It is the garment that will cause the soul to either shine or be obscured. Consider what energy you are producing with that first thought.

As we state below, ninety-five percent of the thoughts a person thinks, and thereby creates angels, on any given day are the same thoughts and angels of yesterday—whether negative of positive—unless he or she decides to think different thoughts. When you wake up every morning, do you think, "Oh, what a beautiful day it is," or, "It's six o'clock, give me five more minutes"? What tone are we setting for our day by having a negative thought first thing in the morning? What if the first thought of our day was:

> "I can hardly wait to see the beautiful blessings that Hashem will bring into my life today!"

If you could muster up to say it with conviction, imagine how much better your day would be because of it. A fantastic technique I learned is to prepare oneself to have that thought in the morning—pre-program the night before that you're going to wake up with said thought in the morning.[13] Say before going to sleep: "**I can hardly wait for tomorrow, when I am going to wake up to great, mystical experiences.**" Then, the next day, after giving thanks to God for

---

[13] The book, *The Miracle Morning*, gives some great advice: One should plan the night before he goes to sleep what his first thought should be in the morning.

restoring your soul with great faith in you, say, "**I can hardly wait for the deep mystical experiences.**"

Beginning of the Week

We begin our week with the ritual of *Havdalah*, with wine, spice, and candle. The spice and candle are meant to give us focus and energy for our coming week. The custom in some synagogues and homes is to laugh after the blessing on wine.[14] The spice is to revive us, given the fact that after Shabbos, our extra soul takes leave from us until the next Shabbos, leaving us feeling somewhat deflated. Looking at the reflection of the candle's flame on our fingernails reminds us of the brilliant, reflected energy of Adam and Chavah before the sin of the Garden of Eden and that we need to be reminded to shoot beyond that.[15]

Beginning of the Year

Starting off right is why it is the custom in every Jewish home to dip the apple in honey on Rosh Hashanah, the beginning of the Jewish year. It is important that we lay a positive foundation for the whole year to come. Just as the ancient Jewish farmer would dedicate his first fruits to Hashem, so it is the Jewish custom to start off the New Year with only positive thoughts, laying a strong, spiritual foundation for the rest of the year.

Beginning of Life

A prime source from the Torah that exemplifies the importance of our thoughts is from when our forefather Yaakov was forced to leave Israel and live with his uncle Lavan. Yaakov's salary in exchange for

---

14 *Kesser Shem Tov, Taamei Haminhagim* 477:12. We laugh to create a good sign and blessing. Also, Rabbi Chaim Palagi (*Nefesh Chaim* 90:23) says to laugh while looking at the fingernails with the candle.

15 See *Taamei Haminhagim* (*Shai Lamora* ed., p. 187), which brings *Pirkei D'Rabi Eliezer*, chap. 14, which states that after eating from the Tree of Knowledge, he saw how he was naked except for his fingernails.

working for Lavan was to marry Lavan's younger daughter, Rachel. He worked seven years for her, after which the wedding was prepared, and yet, a switch was made and Yaakov's father-in-law put Leah, the older sister, in Rachel's place. After the wedding ceremony and feast, Yaakov thought he was having relations with Rachel, but in truth it was Leah.

This thinking, as subtle and unintended as it was, caused a later switch. The offspring of that act was Reuven, the firstborn son of Yaakov. Later, after Rachel died, Yaakov ordered that his bed, which was always in Rachel's tent, be moved to her handmaid Bilhah's tent. When Reuven heard this, his impetuousness got the better of him, and for the honor of his mother Leah, he brazenly entered Bilhah's tent and moved his father's bed into his mother Leah's tent. This seemingly simple move was so significant on his level that the Torah equates it to him lying with his father's wife. For this, he lost the priesthood, as was the custom for all firstborns to serve as the priest of the family.

The switch in the mind of Yaakov precipitated the switch with the bed Reuven moved. In the subtlest ways, Yaakov's thoughts set in motion a situation that was to be manifest later. The *Zohar* says, "**All things go after the thought!**"[16] Of course, this seems very dramatic and even frightening. It almost doesn't seem fair that thoughts should be so important. The level of thinking of our forefather Yaakov was much different from and higher than ours.

But, we say, "the deeds of the fathers are a sign to the children," meaning that the forefathers are compared to the root, and the children are compared to the branches. Whatever happens in the root happens in the branches. The slightest deviations have huge ramifications. Nonetheless, what we must impress upon ourselves is that our thoughts are more powerful than we realize, and we must begin to be aware of them and harness them.

---

16   *Zohar, Bereishis* 168.

Believe it or not, the universe is user-friendly, and the Creator is very patient. So, a person should have faith and know that everything that happens is for the best, even if we are filled with polluted and confusing thoughts. What the *Zohar* wants to illustrate to us is that even though Yaakov had a thought in a different direction unintentionally, it manifested somewhere!

Rabbi Nachman's Teachings on the Power of Thoughts

Know that thought has a very great strength. Even if a person was to strengthen his thoughts that he will have money, then for sure he will get it. This is how it is with everything.

This is only provided, however, that his thoughts will nullify all his feelings [feelings of doubt or fear, for example].

Thought is so powerful that it is possible for one to literally cause his own death with a thought.[17] *Twice a day, we proclaim that God is one with the words, "Hear O Israel! The Lord is our God; the Lord is one." The essential meditation at that time is to be in such a state of love of God that one is willing to give up his life. It is possible to strengthen and make the thought so powerful, such that at the time that the person does this and accepts in his thoughts that he is willing to die for "kiddush Hashem," sanctification for the name of God, he literally feels the pain of death. This is what Rabbi Akiva said, "All my life I was troubled concerning this verse, 'To love Hashem with all your soul,' I would ask myself, 'When*

---

[17] One must keep in mind the idea that placebos work for some people, as well as the evidence from hypnosis where people who were told that something scalding had touched their skin actually formed blisters. There is a story of a person who willed himself to freeze to death when being locked overnight in a commercial freezer. Unbeknownst to him, the freezer was broken.

will this mitzvah come to my hands that I may fulfill it?' and now, I can finally fulfill it!" This means that at the time of the recital of the Shema, Rabbi Akiva accepted upon himself the four death penalties...

So, when a person strengthens his thoughts in giving up his life, he is actually able to die from the pain of that very death that he was contemplating. This is because there is no difference between the actual death and the pain felt from the death in his mind.

Therefore, a person must hold himself back and distance himself in order to remain where he is at the time that he feels so close to passing on, because his soul could permanently leave his body. This is so that he does not die before his time, God forbid.[18]

Conversation #8

When studying subjects dealing with tragedy, like the laws of mourning, do not delve into them too deeply, for our thoughts have great power. Therefore, these subjects should be covered as rapidly as possible.

Conversation #46

Guard your thoughts carefully, for thought can literally create a living thing.[19]

The higher the faculty, the farther it can reach. You can kick something with your foot but throw it higher with your hand. You can reach still farther with your voice, calling to a person very far away. Hearing

---

18 This whole section is from Rabbi Nachman of Breslov, *Likutei Moharan* 1:193.
19 Such as angels!

reaches yet farther, for you can hear sounds like gunfire from a great distance. Your sight reaches even farther, seeing things in the sky.

The higher the faculty, the farther it can reach. Highest of them all is the mind, which can penetrate the loftiest heights. Therefore, you must safeguard your mind very well.

Conversation #62

Human thought has tremendous potential and can bring about many things, even inflation.[20]

When thought is intensely concentrated, it can exert profound influence. Every faculty of the mind, both conscious and unconscious, down to the innermost point, must be focused without distraction. When many people do this, their thoughts can actually force something to take place.[21] To accomplish this, the concentrated thought must spell out every step of the desired result in detail.

However, a diffused, generalized thought is like an incomplete vessel.[22] Such an incomplete mental vessel can lead one to error. This is what happened to Nevat, who saw fire emerging from his circumcision and thought that he would be king.[23] You can also make use of this in your studies. You can focus on something so strongly that it comes true.

---

20 Rabbi Aryeh Kaplan brings a footnote of another passage in *Sichos HaRan* #186, which spoke of a year when there was serious inflation of prices. When there was a good wheat crop that summer, people thought that prices would go down. But the Rebbe said that prices would not go down and that the inflation would last for two years. The Rebbe's prediction came true, and the inflation lasted through the second year. When the two years ended, the prices finally went down.

21 Remember the golden watch incident in the introduction?

22 *Keilim* 12:6. *Chullin* 25a speaks about how vessels, whether wood or metal, can contract uncleanliness only when they are considered completed, but will not contract uncleanliness if they are incomplete.

23 *Sanhedrin* 101b. This error led him to rebel against David Hamelech. Nevat is identified with Sheva ben Bichri, in *Shmuel II* 20. It was actually his son, Yeravam, who became king.

Take, for example, the *Shulchan Aruch*, the Code of Jewish Law. You can calculate that if you study five pages a day from the four sections of the *Shulchan Aruch*, you'll finish all four sections in a single year.

Picture in your mind exactly how you will go about this course of study. Concentrate so strongly that you are completely focused on this thought. If your desire is strong and your concentration intense enough, you will succeed.

CHAPTER THREE
DISCOVERING AND SHIFTING PATTERNS

PATTERNS

We all operate out of patterns—patterns of thinking, speaking, and acting. We have daily routines, habits, and set ways of viewing the world. In the realm of thought, our challenge is that 90–95 percent of the thoughts that we think about ourselves today are the same as those of yesterday. Hence, the type of angels that we were creating yesterday are most likely going to be the same angels that we will create today.

The first step in directing and changing our thoughts, and hence our angels, is to notice those patterns. If we know the pattern, we can be aware of the predictable outcome. Some patterns can be coming from outside triggers. For example, certain noises, songs, odors, or even colors can trigger certain feelings and therefore certain thoughts and behaviors. For example, imagine a small child who is traumatized at a young age when he was brought to a barber for a haircut. The barber had an unusual habit of always snapping his scissors like a chopping machine. To hear the snapping scissors when he was in an already vulnerable state created a link in his brain so that later on in life, whenever he would hear someone snapping scissors, he would get that same negative feeling and even engender a negative behavior. To alter these patterns, we must start to be aware of the various habits of thinking that create certain feelings and therefore certain angels.

The truth is that our evil inclination, which enters into us from birth, has had a twelve- or thirteen-year head start in developing certain patterns in our way of viewing the world and hence our thinking. These patterns have been responsible for all the experiences[1] in our life. We are taught from King David that the service of God consists of two things: "Desist from evil and do good."[2] We have to rectify our negative character traits (including thoughts) as well as actually perform positive actions. We can focus on trying to recognize those negative patterns and attempt to break them, which is a very effective approach. However, I have learned that sometimes the best "desisting from evil" is to create a big good, which means a great positive.[3] This "big good" can come in the form of an action, but any action begins with an empowering thought that will lead to a more creative response. We can spend a lot of energy on the struggle to break the pattern and keep ourselves from falling, but for now, let's try to focus on a fresh style of thinking.

What if, suddenly, all over the world, the keys to all the typewriter keyboards were changed. Suddenly, all the other letters were moved around and were arranged differently from how they are now. If we would want our typing to make sense, we would all have to retrain ourselves to type. And if, while we were in the process of retraining, we were to lose focus for a moment while we were typing, what would happen? We would automatically revert to pressing the keys according

---

1   By experiences, I mean our reactions to things—not what happens to us in the external world, as those come from God.
2   *Tehillim* 34:15. There are two major ways everyone must follow in the service of God. The first is to desist from evil, which means to eradicate bad character traits, bad habits, and (it goes without saying) sinful acts. The second part of the phrase is to "do good," which includes all cultivation of good character traits and positive actions.
3   Many of the Chassidic masters focus on accentuating the positive. To inspire and set ablaze a dynamic path that motivates a person offers to move them away from the negative patterns, which sabotage happiness and joy.

to the old keyboard layout. This is how it is with developing new patterns. It requires faithful focusing until the new pattern is firmly established. Once the new pattern is established and has become acquired, second nature then takes its course, and the pattern becomes automatic.

STIMULUS AND RESPONSE

The very first ethical teaching from Mount Sinai, as stated in *Pirkei Avos*, states: "Be deliberate in judgment." The simple meaning is that this is referring to a judge making a decision of law. However, it seems to me that it is also referring to all people. So, with the understanding that this is addressed to all people, we can get a few relevant insights. One is that we are judging all the time. Isn't that true? The other is that before we do judge, we should wait before responding—to anything! Stop before you judge.[4]

Much has been discussed from self-help books telling us that there is a stimulus, which is what our five senses take in, and then there is our response to that stimulus. In between the stimulus and the response is where our free will lies. We have been endowed with a mind that gives us the ability to wait before responding and choose the highest response. Our holy Kabbalah urges us to be responsible and react with "big brains" as opposed to "small brains," i.e., maturity vs. immaturity.

For example, imagine that you're sitting casually at home relaxing, reading, or engaged in some tranquil activity when you hear a loud crash in the house. All kinds of things go through your mind. What would you be thinking? What would you be feeling? What would you be saying? You quickly rush over to the source of the sound to discover that a member of your household has knocked over a heavy,

---

4   This doesn't mean if action is needed to hold off, as many circumstances require immediate action. What I'm referring to is when you are in a state of judging, our natural state.

expensive vase. Are you relieved or upset? Before your discovery, all kinds of ideas or scenarios were most likely going through your head. Even afterward, discovering that your precious vase is broken will engender a reaction or feeling.

Anyone who has been on the planet for a reasonable length of time can easily see that, when confronted with certain stimuli, they operate in certain patterns.

The big key toward forming new patterns lies in understanding the power of perceptions.

HABITS OF PERCEPTIONS

Perception is nine-tenths of the law; the other tenth is the willingness to see it differently.

Look at this inkblot. What do you see?

First, one must admit that what one person sees, someone else might see differently. It's just an inkblot, abstract and without form. We are not all going to see the same thing. The question is, what makes us see what we see? We can only see in that inkblot things that are based on our own personal experiences or what was taught to us from parents, teachers, friends, etc. **We only bring to the inkblot from our own limited mind.**

If you had never seen a duck-billed platypus in your life, and I would ask you if you could see one in the image above, would you be able to do so? Most definitely not. Since you have never seen one, you would never be able to spot it in the inkblot because we only bring to the inkblot what comes from our own life experience. And now for the bomb…

The truth really is that:

> *All of our experiences are nothing more than an inkblot!*

The reason is because…

We constantly filter all our experiences through our own finite knowledge!

So, just like with the inkblot, where we can clearly see what we bring to each experience from our own limited knowledge, so too, everything that we view in the world is also being filtered through our own limited knowledge and experiences. All of those situations that we encounter are now inkblots with color, depth, and extreme animation. Those encounters even talk back to us!

Does anybody experience the same incident or situation the same way? Even the most evil situation that can be experienced in the world is never met by the exact same frequency vibration reaction. And even if we can say that the two poles of good and evil produce the exact same feeling in everyone, there is a huge gray area in between those two "obvious" poles.

To me, my child is the Divine Presence manifest in innocence and beauty, while from his teacher's perspective, he is anything but an angel.

So, if nobody experiences the same thing the same way, we must ask ourselves:

Where do those feelings come from? One thing for sure is that they don't come from the thing itself! Rather they come from us. They come from our pre-programming.[5]

Now look at the inkblot again and make a demand upon yourself to see something in it that you did not notice before. Turn it sideways or even upside down. Challenge your mind to view it differently.

The essential thing is to know *how much* our perceptions form our experiences. Perceptions engender certain reactions in our nervous system. Hence, our experience. Change our perception, and we can change our experience. Our will and thoughts can affect our perceptions, which, in turn, change our experiences. One merely needs to utilize the creative-thought process and ask the question: "Is there a way to see the situation differently?"

It all comes down to perception! If you change how you view things, then you will alter your internal wiring, and so too your thoughts will change, which will alter your overall experience of that situation! Be deliberate in judgment. Wait! Use your sincere sense of creativity, your ability for a truer broadened perspective. So, if you were to alter your thoughts even slightly, then the angel that you created in the past will be different this time. Hence, you're a new person because you are going in a different direction! You're not the same old guy going along the same old path.

THE COSMIC MIRROR

There is another step to understanding our living, animated inkblot.

The following are different excerpts and adaptations from the teachings of the Baal Shem Tov, along with other sources in our holy writings

---

5   There are two types of programming: inborn and learned. Even inborn programing needs developing. These are patterns that most likely come from past lives and other factors.

that will, hopefully, help the reader integrate this deep, life-changing principle of how everything is a mirror.

> *Shmuel says: "The one who blemishes another surely has that same blemish."*
>
> Kiddushin 70a

In the Talmud, there was a story of a man who was calling various people in the town "slaves." When this was told to the rabbi of the town, Rabbi Yehudah ben Yechezkel, the rabbi pronounced that this person was a slave. The matter was brought to court, and they asked the rabbi, "How do you know?" Whereupon the rabbi answered the above rule—that one who blemishes others indeed has that same blemish. And lo and behold, it was discovered that the man was indeed a slave.

The question was asked: If whoever blemishes or disqualifies another with a certain disqualification, how could it be that the rabbi who proclaimed that he was a slave is not a slave himself? The answer is that when there is a judgment, or what I would call a negative emotional charge, then we say that the person has that blemish. When there is no negative emotional charge, as in the rabbi's declaration, it is not an indication that the person has that blemish.[6]

This is the basic foundation to help navigate this rule in life. If there is a negative emotional charge, then that person has to check themselves out. It does not matter how big or even how small the charge is. A negative emotional charge is a charge. You don't have to get insanely upset. A mere, slight disappointment is an invitation and opportunity from the Creator to grow.

However, those individuals who wish to take it to a much higher level can even ask in the face of such a situation, "Why did God bring me this experience?" "Why did I have to witness this?" Then, that person

---

6   See *Likutei Sichos* from the Lubavitcher Rebbe, vol. 10, pp. 24–29.

can do the introspection and pray that God will reveal to them what they need to develop. Their reason why they do this is because they understand the inclusiveness of all our souls. All Israel is blended, this one with that one.

My father-in-law explained that every one of our souls is a sliver of everyone else's soul.

Who is a wise man? One who learns from every person.
Avos 4:1

It is impossible for a perfectly pure person, who has absolutely no flaws, to see any blemish in anyone or to hear about anyone doing any evil. God will not bring before such a person's eyes any evil and will likewise prevent this person from hearing any evil. Therefore, when a person sees someone who does something wrong or hears about a certain person who did such and such an evil act, he should know clearly that he has within him that same blemish himself. Even if the person seeing or hearing is very saintly, in any case, he has a subtle aspect of that same blemish or flaw.

When I teach this to people, they sometimes fall out of their chair. Many people ask me to repeat it several times because it's so earthshattering.

Now these types of pure people are very hard to come by. I have heard of people who pass away at a very old age, well over a hundred. When asked how the person lived, all those who knew him would respond with comments such as, "He never had a bad word to say about anybody." Some say that when they were with that person, they felt like they were treated as if they were the most important person in the world. Like I said, very few. For the rest of us down here in this world, the implication is obvious. If you do see blemishes in others, you have those same blemishes in some other form or some other degree. This is the understanding of the phrase, "Who is a wise man? He who learns from every person." If you see flaws in others, they are your flaws. So, the Creator is giving you a subtle (or not-so-subtle) reflection of what you need to change. (If that's not God's love, I don't know what is.)

Now you might ask, if I had the experience of witnessing someone stealing, does this imply that I am a thief? For sure, that sounds absurd! But according to the rules of Divine Providence, it is true, though the stealing with which I am involved is in some *other form or degree*. A person must check himself out. Perhaps, he is stealing sleep by building a sukkah[7] on his patio at 2:00 a.m. and waking his neighbors? Perhaps, he is stealing the time of others when he cuts in line? Maybe, he is stealing peace of mind from himself? The Baal Shem Tov is saying that when he sees fault in others, it is likened to one who looks in the mirror and sees his own blemish.[8] So too, the one who sees a blemish in his friend must know that he himself has that blemish in some other form or degree. When a person sees a blemish in the mirror, should he get a hammer and chisel and start bashing the blemish out of the mirror (which is definitely what most people do)? Of course not. Instead, he must fix it in himself. Once he does that, he won't see the blemish in other people.

A story is told about the Baal Shem Tov that he was once in a place where he witnessed people who were profaning the holy Shabbos day. He was shocked that God had brought him such an experience and began contemplating. He sat and went over his entire life, thinking, "Where have I ever profaned the holy Shabbos?" He finally discovered that one time, he asked a Talmudic scholar to perform some menial task on his behalf. He recalled that the Torah calls the Rabbinic scholars

---

7   The booths that Jews live in one week a year. There is a custom to begin building the sukkah immediately after the Yom Kippur fast so as to express eagerness to fulfill the commandments. There might be a tendency to do this mitzvah, including hammering and sawing, even in the middle of the night.

8   *Baal Shem Tov on the Torah, Bereishis* 125.

with the nickname "Shabbos," and so he concluded that it was the source of his blemish, using scholars in a less than honorable way.

This example might be over the top for the rest of us, but for the level of the Baal Shem Tov, it was the right message.

I remember teaching this point to a group of teens one time, and the top student came to me after the class and said what I have heard so often: "I don't buy it. It can't be!" A week later to the day, she came to me again after the class and told me about her conversation with her mother while driving in the car one day. She was complaining about her friend doing such and such, and her mother so casually responded, "That's you sweetie; you do the same thing."

If I see cruelty, then I'm cruel in some other form or some other degree. Whatever it is you see: Experiencing someone obnoxious? Guess what? You're obnoxious. Lazy? That's right. You're lazy.

It also works for the positive. Seeing positive traits displayed is a good reflection. This should rid us of any jealousy issues as well, since what you see in that person is also inside of you. That means it should be so easy to fully rejoice in another's success because it's also your success.

The Baal Shem Tov goes on to further state that when you find this same blemish in yourself and you manage to change it, you will no longer see that blemish in that other person—either the person will be out of your life altogether, or you won't see him that way anymore.

> *In my opinion, we should apply this rule only to those in our direct environment. To hear on the news about some cruel dictator is a tall order, albeit true, and too great a responsibility for us to face. So, we should limit this rule to our local sphere of experience.*

Therefore, I feel that the redemption of the world depends on insights such as these.[9] If we were to behave with this fact deeply embedded in all of our consciousnesses, there would be no more gossip or *lashon hara*.[10] We are taught that our Holy Temple in Jerusalem was destroyed because of baseless hatred and evil speech. If we were to fully grasp this cosmic mirror and altered view of reality, how would we dare think or say something bad about someone knowing that it's our mirror reflection?

So, if we find ourselves getting caught up in a blame game and reacting, "This guy is crazy," or "She is so mean," we must begin to consider, "Why is God sending me this experience?" When we start to realize that it's all a mirror, suddenly all hate and gossip go out the window. It's God reflecting back to us where we need to grow. Not so that we get down on ourselves, God forbid, but because God loves us and wants us to grow. When we all will be aware of this idea and understand it, no one will talk about the flaws of others. If we find ourselves gossiping about so and so, God forbid, those listening will nod their heads and say, "Thank you so much for sharing with me all about yourself." People will take a step back when it comes to outwardly criticizing others for their faults, since they are only expressing their mirror image perception.

So, thus is the rule: "Who is a wise man? One who learns from every person." "Every person" literally includes every person. Accept and allow every person to become your teacher.

---

9   The famous epistle of the Baal Shem Tov relates the journey of the ascent of the soul of the Baal Shem Tov to the hall of the Mashiach. The Baal Shem Tov asked the soul of the Mashiach, "When is the master coming?" and the answer was, "When your teachings are spread about as the wellsprings, and people will be practicing your teachings."

10 The laws of gossip are very detailed and intricate. There are certain circumstances where there is an obligation to speak about others when it meets certain requirements. A competent rabbi should be consulted.

While on the subject of gossip, here is something that the Baal Shem Tov explains on the verse, "Don't be a violent witness against your people." We know from the Torah that one witness is never acceptable in any court, earthly or Heavenly. The rule is that two witnesses are needed to establish something. So, how could the verse express it in the singular, "Don't be a violent witness?" The answer is that if a person, God forbid, speaks badly about anyone, the wicked prosecuting angel, the Satan, drags his soul to be a witness in the Heavenly court to testify against that person's misdeed that he himself spoke about. So now, you together with the Satan are two witnesses, and then a judgment can be made and a sentenced carried out, God forbid.

My wife once took on a project to help a certain family in need. The father was resolved not to live in the city where his children resided. For whatever reason, he threw the responsibility on the community where the children lived to take care of them. Meanwhile, he was partying in another city. I was so angry that this husband and father did not take responsibility for his family. I quickly calmed down, thought of this rule, and said to myself, "You are not taking responsibility for your family!" And, in another form or degree, it was true. I was not guiding my family in the way that I should as far as being there with them to guide them in a Torah path. When I changed my own blemish, this man was gone from my life.

I was once in a synagogue during the holiday of Passover. I was sitting in the back, and it came time for the rabbi's speech. I always try to pay attention and reap an insight, and he was saying wondrous Torah. As the rabbi kept on giving his discourse, I couldn't help being distracted by incessant talking in the back corner. They were rude and brazenly lacking respect for the rabbi and his sharing insights with the community. When their noise became a little too loud, they got hushed down by some others a bit, but they didn't stop talking. I was losing it and if I had something other than a holy prayer book in my hand,

I would for sure have thrown it at them and blasted them with a few words. I kept quiet, however, and said to myself, "Wait, no one else is going nuts about this. How come I'm so bothered about this?" I quickly turned it around, determining in my heart that what they were doing I myself was involved in, in some way or to some degree. "They have no respect for Torah." Really it was me. In another form or degree, I had no respect for Torah. So, I checked inside myself and found where in my life I was not reaching my potential in giving honor to the Torah.

I recall once learning about my own insensitivity from my good friend. He messaged my wife and I that he would be in town for a few days, and I gladly opened my doors for him to stay with us. Then he messaged us that since he will be in town on the festive day of Lag Ba'omer, commemorating the passing of Rabbi Shimon Bar Yochai, author of the *Zohar*, we should have a big party and invite the entire community. He had been in our house and had seen how we operate. We had lost our son to cancer four years prior and had not recovered from it. To throw an event on his whim was simply beyond our capacity. Plus, we had young children who were having health issues at the time, and, of course, our resources were low as a result. "And he wants me to spend money and time and divert energy away from my family to throw him a big party?" I thought. I was incensed. "How insensitive can you be?!" I turned it around and said about myself that I am insensitive. In another form or degree, I was being insensitive to myself, my family, and others. I took a deep breath and saw my friend as being a fantastic teacher.

Another time, one of my children gave me a proverbial smack in the face. At the Shabbos meal, he blatantly called us names that gave me a shock that was extremely unsettling. I was beside myself. Thank You, God, for giving me an opportunity to look at myself. My reaction to my child was, "I owe you nothing! You live in my house, eat my food, etc. You are not recognizing the good that we are giving you." I instantly thought to myself, "I'm not recognizing the good that God is giving me!" And in so contemplating, I worked on developing a deeper recognition of God, Who owes **me** nothing.

> *It is not good for man to be alone; I will make for him a helper against him.*
>
> Bereishis 2:18

Here is another source with some additional insights.

This verse is simply understood as expressing the idea that God wanted to bring Adam a wife. The Baal Shem Tov brings out a bit more:

> *If he was by himself, then he would think that he is a totally devout and perfect person. This is the explanation of "it is not good for man to be alone," because he will never be able to see his faults and where he needs to grow. Therefore, "I will make him a helper that comes from that which is against him" (literally facing him, like a mirror). All this [is] in order that he should realize that he has that sort of blemish to some degree or form…*
>
> *When you see something that is ugly from your friend, first feel that it is for your good. Determine for yourself that you have some of that same shortcoming. Then return to your thoughts and recognize that it is for your good.*
>
> *Therefore, if a person's prayers become disturbed or confused by some "wicked neighbor" who only seeks to disturb him and stop him from praying correctly or learning or otherwise, the first thing to consider is that it is for his specific good to instruct him about the way of praying with the proper intention and that this "agent" was sent to inform him about his levels of concentration in order that he should become even stronger. May the wise man hear and reap.*

And of course, believe it or not, this is directly regarding one's spouse. One's spouse is a mirror reflecting what they need to address within themselves! The challenge is to really do the work. There might be some people, God forbid, who choose to deny this rule and choose to crawl back to their pathetic caves and live a life of sorrow and misery. That's a thought pattern all on its own. If you are contemplating this, God forbid, then I refer you back to chapter one.

I have, however, found a place where this rule might not apply.

Moshe and the Sin of the Golden Calf

"And if You cannot forgive them, then erase me from Your book!" These were the words of Moshe, our teacher, when he prayed on behalf of the Jewish People after the sin of the golden calf. At first glance, it seems pretty audacious for the humblest man in existence to make such a bold threat. Actually, it was not a threat of any kind, God forbid. Rather, Moshe was assuming responsibility, contemplating whether he was to blame for the golden calf. "Perhaps, a thought of idolatry came into my mind, and I did not eradicate it fast enough or in the right way? So that, in a certain sense, since I am the leader, I caused this to happen through my thoughts."[11] Therefore, "Erase me from Your book." God quickly answered him and said that he is not to blame. The point here is that he had the experience of this beloved people commit idolatry and looked into himself. God had to tell him, "Stop looking!" Here we see the rule and its exception. I don't see how anyone other than a prophet can exclude himself, as only God Himself could tell someone to stop looking.

---

11 See *Baal Shem Tov in the Torah, Parashas Ki Sisa*, where he explains the rule that the leader of the community has spiritual influence on the community. One small thought that is not eradicated from his mind will bleed into the minds of the populace and influence them. For those spiritually stronger, it might manifest as a thought, while for those of weaker faith, it expresses itself as an actual forbidden act, such as the golden calf.

Rabbi Meir and the Hoodlums

There were certain hoodlums who lived in the same neighborhood as Rabbi Meir, a Sage from the times of the Mishnah. Rabbi Meir's initial response was to pray that the hoodlums be destroyed. His holy wife, Beruria, rebuked him, saying that, rather, he should entreat the Blessed Holy One that they should realize their evil path and revert their ways.

Agreeing with his wife, he did so, and the hoodlums changed their ways.

The classic Talmudic commentator known as the *Maharsha* asks the question, "How could his prayer affect them? Free will is Creation's most important ingredient that can never be abrogated!" I would propose the possibility that what he prayed for was the aspect in himself that these hoodlums were manifesting. Of course, Rabbi Meir was, as Shlomo Carlebach would say, "the highest of the highs, the deepest of the deep," yet he knew in a very subtle, minuscule way that there was something in the deepest recesses of his heart on the most basic level. Otherwise, God would not cause him to experience that. So, praying on the aspect within himself led to the experience of the hoodlums in his midst to return to the kosher path.

Don't Judge a Person until You're in His Place

And the truth is you never will be in that person's place, so it's best not to judge. Besides, according to the rule above concerning our cosmic mirror, you are only judging yourself.

The real, wilder scenario about judging is that you are actually signing your own sentence and sealing your own fate when you judge.[12] That's right! Heaven can only collect on a balance due when

---

12 For a discussion on this precise point, see *Sefer Baal Shem Tov, Parashas Kedoshim* (*Vayikra* 19:15, point 5).

the person himself, on a soul level, agrees. That's how it works. So, how does Heaven get the person to agree? They bring someone who does what you do in a different form or degree. He is in your range of consciousness and in the sphere of your senses. You see it and judge that person. When that happens, you have just signed your own judgment! Simple solution: stop judging. Yes, be concerned for the person. Yes, pray for him. Guide him if you have the ability. But, most of all, pray for yourself when you find yourself in that situation. Ask God why He put you in that situation. Ask God why you have such negative feelings. Go to the Source and stop trying to chisel out the blemish in the mirror.

Perception of Self—Overcoming Our Sense of Inadequacy

Looking in the mirror of one's faults is not meant to lead one to narcissism and certainly not depression. It's meant to lovingly lead us to grow. After realizing that our experience of others is an opportunity to see ourselves, we'll know clearly who we really are, and, ultimately, heal.

> *We are a soul, and our body is merely a garment.*

We are carved from the Unlimited Creative Intelligence Whom we call God. We have power and abilities of which we are not even aware. Just as a baby eagle that is brought to a chicken coop and starts to peck like chickens simply because it doesn't know what it is, so too, we behave in the limited way to which we were exposed. We have unlimited capabilities and desperately need to awaken to whom we really are. However, even though we can understand our mission to be woken up to who we really are, we still have to deal with our sense of inadequacy.

Our sense of inadequacy is not a new issue but goes all the way back to the desert when the Jewish People tested God ten times.[13] There was a group of people, known as the *eirev rav*, mixed multitude, who tagged along with the Jews in the desert. They attached themselves to the Jewish People and sought to influence those who were of weak faith and prompted them to complain. Also, the other times in which the Jews complained were instigated by only a few people and not everyone—whether it was for water, for meat, or the bread from Heaven called *manna*, which they didn't appreciate. Ten complaints, including the golden calf and the incident of the spies, the latter of which caused the Jewish People to wander in the desert for forty years.

The question was asked, "If it was only a few people and the *eirev rav* who instigated such tumult, why is it considered that the entire nation was testing God?" The answer is that the Jewish People felt so inadequate because God was constantly showering abundant love upon them; they couldn't take it. They couldn't believe it, saying, "It can't be that God could be with us like this!" They were brought out of Egypt with open miracles, fed bread from Heaven, watered from a rock, and protected by clouds. The love was overwhelming. So, they tested God as a result of their own inner sense of inadequacy. They let those of weak faith instigate their rebellion and stood by silently. Their silent agreement was coming from their place of inadequacy.

Truly, our final healing and rectification will be out acceptance of this great love in a way that we can take it. We must integrate clearly and deeply who we are and what our purpose is in the world. To love and appreciate our connection to the Infinite in the very state in which we are. This is where all our efforts must work toward. This is the real work of *emunah* (faith), and we fail because we don't believe it. One of the biggest leaps of *emunah* is to believe in ourselves. We each have

---

13 *Leshem Shevo V'Achlamah, Sefer Hade'ah*, part 2.

our own very unique soul frequency tune that we must access and play. And play it with boundless joy we must.

The point for now is to realize that we are really a Divine soul in a garment body, and we must live with this idea. The topic of correct self-love is such a huge topic that it deserves its own study. I'm just introducing the idea that since perception is so important, our perception of ourselves needs serious overhaul.

Try this exercise: Get up and walk around the room, affirming this thought: "I am a soul, and my body is a garment."

The thing that heals our inner sense of inadequacy will be that we will finally get that it's not about us; it's about God's expression. We need to embrace our total vulnerability and dependency with love; to focus with the right intention; to merely be a conduit for God's unlimited expression; to only seek and yearn for God's expression.

> "God, my only desire is for the full expression of Your infiniteness to be manifest for all, right here and now."

> "I am now allowing infinity to manifest its infiniteness by means of me. All inadequacy is gone—because I am only receiving it for the sake of the expression of that infiniteness."

Love Your Neighbor as Yourself

It's interesting how the basic premise of this prime directive seems to have been in exile. Everybody understands the "love your neighbor" part of the phrase. It's the "as yourself" part that gets kind of fuzzy. From the simple reading of the verse, it seems the "as yourself" part is the known and the given; it's a reference. How much do you love your neighbor? As much as you love yourself.

So, the assumption is that you love yourself. Is it a true assumption? I've met some people who don't seem to have a genuine love of themselves. They either dislike the way they look or the way they act. They have a bad habit or, perhaps, their lives in general are to their disliking. Perhaps they accept who they are since they have no choice, but they wish that they were someone else. Since they don't like these external elements of their being, they therefore seem to be not really loving themselves. Where do we acquire this genuine self-love?

Some will say, "Of course, you love yourself! Everybody loves themselves." Or do they? In what way? Maybe they love themselves through the typical, selfish, self-centered mentality? This type of self-love only leads to emptiness and sadness.

The simple understanding of the verse is to look out for the physical needs of others as you would look out for your physical needs. As people will naturally take care of their own needs, so too, they must seek out and make sure that their fellow's needs are also taken care of. If one cannot fulfill it in actuality, he should, nevertheless, have the strong desire to look out for the needs of others.

A deeper understanding is that people will love themselves despite their faults. They might be disappointed with themselves if they fell into a bad habit, or get angry at themselves if they made a mistake, but in a week or so, they will find a way to forgive themselves and work toward finding a reason to go on living.[14] The reason for this is the well-known idiom, "Love covers all sins." We eventually let it go and find ways to give ourselves the benefit of the doubt. So too, we must love our friend even though we see faults in him (which, as noted above, really mean my own faults that I'm seeing in him). This is why it says

---

14 The Izhbitzer Rebbe, *Mei Shiloach, Parashas Kedoshim*.

at the end of the verse, "I am God." I love both of you. Even though I definitely see your faults, you are both My children.

We can begin to have an appreciation for ourselves. We are a soul, and our body is a garment. The body is a garment that includes all our bad habits, character traits, and craziness. Once we realize this, it becomes a lot easier to tolerate ourselves. All that stuff is exterior clothing that does not dictate what my inner essence is! It is external and will eventually be "shaken off."

There is a pervasive attitude in the world such that most people believe they have little value. They might think, "God doesn't care about my prayers and good deeds." Nothing can be farther from the truth!

Acquiring genuine self-love comes from internalizing how much God loves each and every one of us. We are His children, and that can never be changed. The "given" to which the Torah is referring to is the love of ourselves in the sense of value. I have value; that's the given! The proof of that is that I am alive today, and God has great faith in me. (We say it every morning when we rise; it's too bad that most don't really integrate this.)

> *Take a moment to realize and feel the abundant love that your Infinite Creator has for you and how much He believes in you—that you can accomplish anything.*

Thank God for the holy masters who constantly guide us to retrieve our true selves. The retrieving goes all the way back to Avraham our forefather, the first Jew. Avraham was the first to bring a level of God-awareness into the world that had been absent since the sin of the Garden of Eden. He championed the idea of one God and, within that, the idea that God loves His creation and that we have tremendous value.

The world couldn't take what Avraham was professing, so they tried to destroy him. Most people have some resistance to this idea and are uncomfortable with it. I feel that this is an essential part of our holy Torah that has been there all along yet has not been emphasized. That's what I call the Torah in exile. Funny how loving yourself gets so overlooked.

Rabbi Nachman—Law 282

I asked my mentor, Rabbi Dovid Selzer, "What is the crux of the teachings of Breslov?"

He answered me, "Spiritual Law 282; go look there."

Law 282 brings the adage of judging everyone on the balance of merit. Rabbi Nachman takes it to a whole new level. He begins by discussing a person who we would view as a wicked person. He instructs us that we should use our power of perception and seek in that person a good point. Somewhere, there must be some good point within that person, and with our power of perception and focus on that one good point, we can actually elevate that person! Our power of perception affects that person. Powerful.

Then he goes on to direct us to look and find the good points in ourselves. It's not only important to see the good in ourselves so that we don't fall into depression, but it's also for us to attune to and discover our special melody. We are supposed to gather our own unique good points, one after the other, and continue to gather them more and more. That builds our personal melody. We all have a unique soul frequency and mission that no one else in all of Creation, past or present, can express. It is our unique mission, and many holy books speak about it.[15]

---

15   *Sanhedrin* 37a states that every individual is required to say, "For me the world was created."

Perception of Our Challenges

Everything comes from Heaven, except fear of Heaven.

Berachos 33b

There are two kinds of experiences that Heaven will send us. The first kind of experience is when God reflects back to us who we are and what we are doing. Hence, we are taught that everything that God does is measure for measure. This is the cosmic mirror.

The second kind of experience we will call "*nisayon,*" which literally translates as "test," but really means "expressing your potential."[16]

The situations of our daily experience fly in our face. How we react to them is our free choice. The bottom line is that we have free will regarding every reaction. One must accept the situations in which he finds himself and with a feeling of being loved, asking, "Why is the Unlimited Creative Intelligence sending this situation to me? The Infinite is definitely coaching me to a higher plane by teaching me something about myself." Our reactions to situations come from us. Some people get a flat tire and shake it off. Most people, however, are irritated when such a thing happens. Of course, having *emunah* is the key to our experiences, and this is the real understanding of the adage, "Everything comes from Heaven, except fear of Heaven." We have all been taught the more common translation of the phrase "…except fear

---

See the Slonimer Rebbe's *Nesivos Shalom* 1:6 on living your destiny (*yi'ud* in Hebrew). See Arizal, *Shaar Hakavanos*, section two, how no prayer a person makes one time is equal to another time or day for him or any other person who ever existed, past, present, or future.

16 See Rabbi Eliyahu Dessler, *Michtav M'Eliyahu* 1:12–13 (*Strive for Truth*, pp. 59–60). The root of the word in Hebrew has three meanings: test, banner, and miracle. The common denominator is that they are things that stick out. They reveal something that, now, can be seen. Banners are raised high, miracles are revealed providence above nature, and tests bring out a person's hidden potential. See *Kli Yakar, Bamidbar* 22:12.

of Heaven," but the real understanding, as explained by the *Zohar*, is that instead of "fear," read "*emunah*."[17]

EMUNAH—THE BEST AND ONLY REACTION

Everything that I have just written is just explaining *emunah* in another way. *Emunah* is loosely translated as faith or belief, but it means so much more. Rabbi Lazer Brody simply defines it as "connection to God." Everyone in the world who has his hand on the pulse of the challenges of the times cannot stop talking and writing about them. We need to develop a pattern of thinking where we react with awareness and complete belief that everything that happens comes from the Creator Who loves us—to know that whatever it is, it is for our best and to pray, "Please God, help me to accept it with love!" This is truly the most special and only thing that we can bring to the table. It is our job and destiny to have faith, as the prophet said concerning the end of days, "The righteous man lives on faith."[18]

There are so many books on faith these days, and more and more come out all the time. It's OK if, or when, you realize that they are all saying the same thing just in different ways. It's all part of retraining a new pattern of thinking; a sort of reprogramming our minds. It needs constant integration.

THE WAGER TO MAKE HILLEL ANGRY

There is a passage in the Talmud that speaks of two people who made a bet for a considerable sum of money regarding which of them could

---

17   *Zohar, Parashas Vayeira*. When confronted about why Avraham told everyone that Sarah was his sister, Avraham told Avimelech, "There is no fear of God in this place, and you would kill me." The *Zohar* explained it as *emunah*. Also, Rabbi Yisrael Salanter, founder of the Mussar Movement, specifically explained our adage to be referring to *emunah*.
18   *Chavakuk* 2:4.

anger the great sage, Hillel. One decided to accept the bet and waited for Friday afternoon when Hillel was bathing.

> *He came to the door, shouting, "Where is Hillel! Where is Hillel!"*
>
> *Hillel got out, covered himself, and kindly asked the man if he could help him in any way.*
>
> *The man said, "I have a question."*
>
> *"Ask, my son, ask," replied the Sage.*
>
> *"Why do Babylonian people have strange-shaped heads?"*
>
> *Hillel responded, "Such a good question! It's because of having inexperienced midwives involved in the birth process, so the children get strange-shaped heads in the birth canal."*
>
> *He left and came back a little while later and asked another question, "Why do Tarmudian people have round eyes?"*
>
> *Hillel answered in the same tone, responding, "That's a big question," saying that it was because they live in a sandy place where winds blow frequently.*
>
> *The man left and came back a third time, "Where is Hillel? I have a question." When Hillel came, he asked him, "Why do Africans have wide feet?"*
>
> *Hillel responded, "That's a great question! Because they live in a swampy area."*
>
> *Then the person finally admitted that he made a bet with someone, and that he'd lost the bet because Hillel didn't get angry with him. Hillel said, "It is better for you to lose four hundred zuzim than for Hillel to get angry."*[19]

---

19 *Shabbos* 30b–31a.

The *Maharsha* asks, "This person came with ridiculous questions. Why is Hillel responding to him every time with 'Great question'?"

The answer is that Hillel's perception was completely different.

Rather, Hillel actually had a different experience. He viewed this as an opportunity to bring light into the world. In *his* perception, each one of those questions was a deep question related to a Torah principle, and his answers matched those questions!

Hillel understood that this person was asking about the three evil character traits: an inflated spirit, the evil eye, and a big ego. The first question about the head shape of the Babylonians was inquiring about the sin of the leaders in Babylon who had lost their wealth. Hillel responded that the reasons the "Babylonians' heads were rolled" was because they didn't have "*chayos pikchos*," literally smart midwives, but another interpretation is that their inflated spirit overpowered them, and their wits didn't have life energy, i.e., they lost their wits because anyone with pride is considered an imbecile and out of his mind. Although the person came to Hillel with one thing in mind, Hillel understood the question to be about something completely different.

In conclusion, we must integrate into our mindset this idea that our perceptions create so much of what we experience. There is always a different way to look at things, and just that understanding can propel us to create a higher experience.

CHAPTER FOUR
EXPANDING OUR MEASURE
UTILIZING CAUSE AND EFFECT

God is your shadow.
Tehillim 121:5

EVERYTHING GOD DOES is measure for measure.

It's referred to as tit-for-tat, karma, "what goes around comes around," "you reap what you sow," etc. But in Torah terms, we call it "measure for measure," meaning that God will bestow upon you in the same way and in the same measure that you treat other people and situations. "God is your shadow." The Baal Shem Tov explained this rule from the verse "You shall love your neighbor as yourself; I am God."[1] Move the punctuation so that it reads: "Love your neighbor; as you are, I am God." The direct understanding is that "God is your shadow." Just as your shadow moves with you, so does God. As an individual behaves with his fellow man, such as with compassion and love, so too, Heaven will behave that way with the individual. But it's much deeper than that, since it effects into the area of thought and beliefs.

---

1   *Vayikra* 15:18. The simple way to read the verse is how the world reads it: "Love your neighbor as yourself. I am God."

The source that the Talmud brings for the principle of measure for measure is quite remarkable.[2] We learn it from the story of Elisha the Prophet in *Sefer Melachim*. There was an Israelite city that was besieged by an enemy, which of course brought extreme famine to the city to the point where women were eating their own children. The king finally humbles himself to call in the prophet for a remedy.

The prophet Elisha stated, "Tomorrow, wheat will be sold in the market for a dollar a pound."

The chief of the army exclaimed, "If God were to make windows in the heavens, can such a thing happen?"

Elisha answered him, "You will see it with your own eyes, but you will not eat from it!"

A miraculous event occurred. Some starving lepers who were stuck just outside the city walls figured to go and give themselves up to the enemy camp. "What do we have to lose?" they thought. "If they kill us, we are dead already, but maybe we can at least become prisoners and eat a meal." They came to the camp and discovered that it was completely abandoned with all the army's provisions for the taking. What happened was that the enemy army that was surrounding the city suddenly heard noises from afar and unanimously concluded that it was other armies coming to help Israel.[3] So, the entire army fled in panic. The lepers felt this was too good to hold back and told everyone in the besieged city. So, people went and brought the provisions back to the city. Lo and behold, wheat wound up selling for a dollar a pound! So, the king's captain went and saw, but wound up being trampled by the starving crowd. Just as Elisha had said, the chief of the army only

---

2   *Sanhedrin* 90a.
3   That's right, God can get into the minds of anyone and lead them to believe anything. See the Aramaic translation of the verse after, "My strength and might got me my success" (*Devarim* 8:17): God put the advice in your mind to follow that business endeavor.

saw the wheat selling for that price, but he did not partake of it. He was fed his own disbelief.

So, we see from this source that the measure-for-measure principle includes thoughts and beliefs as well.

Consider for a moment the notion of our beliefs and how they create our reality. How much does our limited style of thinking affect our experiences in life? We must realize that God is our shadow! If we don't believe that we can have it all, then we get to choose how much less of it all that we can have.

> *There is nothing God cannot do by means of me; by means of us.*

The well-known incident of the spies, found in the *Sefer Bamidbar*, relates the situation of twelve spies going into the Land of Israel before the conquest. All but two came back with a bad report. In their evil report of the Land of Israel, they exclaimed, "The people there are giants…we were grasshoppers in our own eyes, and so we were in their eyes."

Taking note of the double language of the text, "**we were** in our eyes like grasshoppers, and so **we were** in their eyes," the commentaries explain that the degree of self-value of the spies was what gave rise to their experience. The Gemara relates that the spies related an actual incident whereby they were spotted in a garden by the giants in the land, at which point the giants exclaimed, "Look, there are ants in the garden that look like people!"[4] Their sense of self-inadequacy in themselves gave rise to their actual, external experience. There are many more texts and concepts that bring out this concept. The verse

---

4   *Sotah* 35a.

from *Tehillim*, "God is your shadow,"[5] also expresses the concept that everything God does is measure for measure.

I know a person who was very upset with us, and we couldn't find out why. He had turned a cold attitude toward us, and we finally couldn't stand it anymore and asked him, "What is it that's bothering you?" He finally admitted and called us out on something that we did, exclaiming that we overlooked him. Through the wording in a social media post, we didn't mention him, so he felt overlooked. We truly had no intention of overlooking him, but he was greatly agitated and expressed it to us. We realized only later, noticing all his live experiences, that he had an agenda of being overlooked. Otherwise, he would never have had that reaction.

> *The world treats you the way that you treat you.*

This principle of measure for measure is not infallible.

We are taught that there are two forms of how God manifests His Divine providence: the "guiding force of balance" and the "guiding force of Oneness."[6] The guiding force of balance is measure for measure. The guiding force of Oneness is what I call "special treatment" or the "unknowable agenda."

The guiding force of Oneness always acts as an executive override. No matter what we do or how we think, there are some decrees that cannot be changed. A person might still think the loftiest, most positive, and happiest thoughts when they're sick, and yet might still die. This higher agenda guarantees that there is an even higher reality to

---

5   *Tehillim* 121:5.
6   Rabbi Moshe Chaim Luzzatto, *Daas Tevunos* 166:4, *Hanhagas Hayichud*.

reach—a higher concept to grasp, a Oneness to which the Unlimited Creative Intelligence is bringing us. The bottom line is: You just have to trust your knowledge of the Unlimited Creative Intelligence Who is directing the universe to its highest experience. And we are just too limited to figure it out right now.

When my brother, *a"h*, passed away from non-Hodgkin's lymphoma, my father exclaimed, "Who said a healing has to come in the form of the body healing?" The word *tikkun* in Hebrew literally means rectification, but I have seen it also translated as healing—a healing that can traverse a lifetime. A healing of soul. Our souls can go through several lifetimes, and the Unlimited Creative Intelligence brings us situations in each of them to bring us to final completion. In the end, the Creator will show us how all of the situations in our lifetime and reincarnations made sense. However, because we are stuck in this limited plain, most of us are clueless. So, in the larger scheme of the process of the soul, it could be seen as a healing in a higher sense.

The Creator's agenda is to make us into vessels that will receive the Infinite Light. His purpose will be fulfilled. If we fully integrate that agenda into the deepest fibers of our being, if we truly understand what God is doing, and if we totally grasp His Divine providence, we would feel very differently when adversity strikes.[7] As stated previously, it all comes down to trusting the Infinite One. For example, when a doctor performs a procedure that is painful or uncomfortable, the patient accepts it because he knows that it will make him better.

We can try and understand this with a parable: You're in a car with a driver Who happens to be…God. "How do you like My driving?" Sometimes, the trip is smooth and moves just as planned, or at least somewhat predictable, while sometimes your ride is completely off the

---

7   The highest response would be to accept all things with love. It is a true art to develop, and all the righteous and knowing people constantly work on this.

wall and the Driver appears to be going off a cliff! Maybe He is driving in a bad neighborhood or in the opposite direction according to your feeble, limited comprehension. Sometimes, the Driver will stop the car, take a beloved family member and throw him out before continuing on, leaving them in the dust. Sometimes, He will let some interesting people on who will harass or annoy you in some way. Those can be trying times and force you to choose to either trust the Driver or argue with Him. If you trust in the Driver, then you can relax and enjoy the ride. Once we fully integrate that God is running the world and there is a goal in mind, we can at least attempt to be a little more at ease.

AWAKENING FROM ABOVE—AWAKENING FROM BELOW

Our free choice offers us a unique opportunity to co-create *how* we would like to become a vessel that experiences and marvels in the infinite light. In the end, we will become that vessel.[8] This opportunity presents itself in the form of two schools: the school of wisdom and the school of "hard knocks," i.e., trial and error. The school of wisdom begins with learning from others, resulting in higher thinking and higher faith. The school of hard knocks is when we don't wake ourselves up to our mission and we need an "awakening from Above." The awakening from Above usually, but not always, comes as an uncomfortable experience. This is in order to get the Creation to realign itself on the path to growth.

In other words, we can either expand our consciousness to develop a loving and trusting relationship with the Unlimited Creative Intelligence Who made us, or we can choose to get beaten into the beautiful vessel to which we are all in the process of becoming.

---

8   That's right. God always gets what He wants.

You either climb the ladder yourself or get starkly encouraged into climbing it regardless.

Whether we like it or not, we are all in the process of becoming vessels to receive the infinite light. If we stay small-minded, we will eat those consequences. So, we might as well be big-minded and work to expand our consciousness as much as we can.

The ultimate expanded thought is to put all the aspects of our lives in the hands of our Infinite Creator and feel a hundred percent secure about it. Directing our thoughts is our best effort. One must keep in mind, however, that even if they have all their thoughts in complete alignment, the outcome is still not guaranteed. There is always the "Higher Agenda." Also, one should not feel pressured saying, "Oh no! What if I don't have the right thoughts?" Remember to take it "easy." We must keep the attitude that the universe is "user friendly." God is very patient. If we stay with the program, even if we exert just the minimum amount of effort, God says that our thoughts create our reality.

But, it could be overridden any second. There is no nature. God is doing all of the driving. We might be thinking that we are involved somewhat, but it's like a child in the car with his little toy steering wheel. When dad or mom turn the wheel, the child turns it and thinks that the car is turning because of him. So, one might ask, why do anything since God is doing it all? The effort we must make is in choosing the school of wisdom to come to trust and know God through the discipline of reaching for the highest thoughts.

> *"Thank You, God, for making it so easy to put my life in Your hands, and thank You, God, for giving me the opportunity to put a hundred percent trust in You!"*

INFINITY HAS YOUR BACK

Let's examine Newton's third law of motion, which states that for every action, there is an equal and opposite reaction.

The swinging balls in the image demonstrate Newton's third law of motion. What happens when I pull just one of the balls back and let it go? It will swing and strike the other balls, resulting in one ball swinging out from the other side. If, instead, I pull back two balls and release them to strike the other motionless balls, so then two balls will swing out the other side. It gets a little more puzzling when I pull back three or four balls, leaving two or one stationary. What do you think happens? As we see from experience, if you pull back four balls and there is only one ball remaining, the result is that four balls will come out swinging from the other side. This mechanism demonstrates the principle that for every action, there is an equal and opposite reaction.

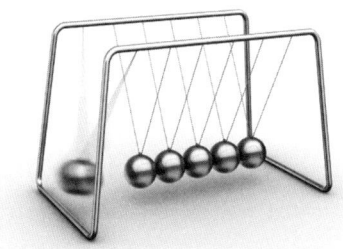

For our purposes, this law of motion translates into the rule of: "According to the effort, so is the reward." People come to me all the time because they don't get enough attention from their spouse, or they want more money, peace of mind, etc. The rule is that to the degree that we give those things, so we will receive them. You want love? Give love. You want sustenance? Give sustenance. You want wisdom? Give wisdom. Just as the force of those swinging balls striking the dormant one elicits a reaction, so too must we swing into action and give what we want to receive. I don't know if this rule works in all areas, but until one has genuinely tried it, they have no one to blame except themselves.

From this rule, we can also get a deeper understanding of how *emunah* works. How many times in life do we find ourselves staring at one dormant single ball—be it in our relationships, our livelihood, or really anything? It doesn't seem like much is going to happen. The only thing we see in the "real" world is one ball. Yet, according to the demonstration above, if four balls were to hit it, the manifestation would be four balls in motion instead of one stationary ball. To me, this alludes to a great power of awakening and belief.

Imagine that there is a place where there are unlimited balls, an unlimited power waiting to be unleashed, despite the fact that we see only one motionless ball before us. Stop and think. Where are you coming from? Are we coming from limited-style thinking or unlimited-style thinking? Do you believe that the Creator has your back? If you believe that He does, then He will.

> *No matter how the situation appears to you,*
> *if you come at it with the force of Infinity,*
> *there is nothing that can stop the reaction*
> *that can be manifest.*

To the degree of the awakening from below, so is the bestowal from Above.[9] To put it another way: Don't come to God with a Dixie cup.

The awakening within us has tremendous power. We just have to do it. The examples of this are numerous. When Moshe was sent by God to bring the Jewish People out of Egypt, he first went to the Jewish People and told them that God had sent them and that the time of the redemption has now arrived. Then he went to Pharaoh. Sure, in a normal storyline, you're going to tell the poor, oppressed victim that

---

9   *Kedushas Levi, Parashas Beshalach.*

he is going to be saved and then go knock out the door of the bad guy. But our holy Torah is much deeper than that. It's not about nice stories. It must have a practical dynamic for our souls in the here and now. So, the Kabbalists explain that the reason why Moshe went first to the people and then to Pharaoh is because there was a need to awaken the Jewish People first. Only then could he go to the Egyptian king and move the redemption forward. He understood that building a vessel is necessary in order for God to bestow something into that vessel. The awakening below builds that vessel. The thoughts of awakening create such a force that no matter what the appearances are, things beyond can manifest.

> "There is nothing that God cannot do by means of me. Thank You, God, for opening me up to be that expanded vessel!"

UTILIZING THE ZONE OF "AZ"

Another example comes from the miracle of the parting of the Red Sea. We are taught that the sea did not split until a man from the tribe of Yehudah went into the sea and the water went up to his nose. That man was Nachshon ben Aminadav. Moshe was directed by God to stop praying and take action. So, Nachshon did exactly that. One Chassidic commentator asks, what was he thinking? Was he moving himself to self-sacrifice as many Jews have done in the past, committing himself to die? Or was he anticipating a miracle? The answer is that he was anticipating a miracle!

The word "*az*" in Hebrew means "then" in future tense. He was exclaiming to himself as he was walking into the water, "Then we are going to sing about this!"—for the same reason Miriam and the group of women easily pulled out tambourines and started singing. Pretty amazing that they brought them in the first place, let alone that they didn't have to go through ten suitcases until they found them. Yes, Miriam and all the other women brought their musical instruments because they anticipated wonders.

The same is true about King David. Before he would go out to war, he would sing praises in anticipation of winning the battle, which were all part of the awakening below, what I call the *quantum thought*; see chapter seven. I call it the *"Az Zone,"* on which we will elaborate on in chapter six. The incident at the Red Sea was where the final redemption from Egypt occurred. When God brought the ten plagues upon Egypt, that was in the category of "awakening from Above." However, that kind of awakening does not facilitate a complete redemption. The element that was needed for the final redemption from Egypt did not occur until there was an "awakening from below," and that did not happen until Nachshon went walking right into the sea with the belief in the miracle!

> *Besides Pharaoh's charging chariots, prayer is the ultimate form of awakening.*

There is one area in Torah technology that lends itself to cause and effect, and that is prayer, but perhaps not the prayer you know or to which you have been accustomed. The Hebrew root for prayer is *"pallel,"* which means to think or to judge. What are we thinking? What are we judging? We think first what we want, and then we judge why we want it. So much goes into this and so much has been written about the subject of prayer, but we only want to touch on one aspect.[10]

---

[10] See chapter seven for a more expanded explanation of this subject.

The crux of prayer as explained by the holy masters comes from the question: "How can we change God's opinion or decree?" The verse states, "I am God; I do not change." How does our prayer affect God to "change His mind," so to speak? The answer is really that through prayer, we don't change God's mind, but rather, we change ourselves!

Prayer builds our vessel. Our experiencing a lack or a struggle is a call to reach for the higher, more expanded vessel.

We are taught that every blade of grass has an angel standing above it, striking it and saying "grow." How much more so must we as creations have angels smacking us and saying the same thing! There are certain species of crabs that feel pressure at certain stages in their growth. They have to crawl under a rock and shed their shell in order to look for a bigger shell. Having to shed their old shell and find a new one is a sign of growth. When we are in a tight spot, it's a sign that we need to reach a higher "shell," a higher vessel.

My *rebbi*, Rabbi Mordechai Goldstein, once called prayer the "aerobics of the will." Prayer is about focusing our attention and our will. Our will forms who we really are and brings us to focus on what we really want. One must practice daily in order to have an open dialogue with his Creator. The obstacles to this type of prayer might seem big, but we know from our demonstration of the swinging balls that it means nothing. Your twenty-four-hour day might seem like one small ball, but with the force of the soul, its power can't be limited. Prayer helps us awaken ourselves before we need an awakening from Above. All those awakenings in our lives that we have experienced from Above are good in the end. When we find ourselves in the middle of such awakenings, however, we might be a tad far away from greeting them with a gleeful smile and appreciating their goodness. From the outward appearances, they can seem to be only trouble and pain, except, perhaps, to those very few whose *emunah* is very strong, even during dark times.

Everything in our life is an effect for which there is a cause. Things don't happen by accident. The originating cause to everything that happens in life comes from God, which is why I refer to God as the "Unlimited Creative Intelligence." The reason is because saying the name God can carry all kinds of mixed or contorted feelings and implications.

We need to tickle our brains a little and offer other descriptions for the purpose of reaching outside the dots.

Your past experiences and learned or adopted beliefs form your perceptions and how you look at things. These beliefs are responsible for how you experience situations in your life.

All those effects or situations in your life are your experiences, and how you experience these situations depends upon what you are aware of and what your beliefs are. If you believe it's not all from the Creator, then you believe your experience is from the Creator **and** something else. If you believe it's something outside of the Creator, then, measure for measure, the Creator leaves you to that "other," and good luck with that, because that "other" is limited and therefore has no source of its own.

Your consciousness—which is your belief system, your ideas, and the thoughts you entertain—goes before you, compelling you to create the conditions in your life that are in harmony with the level of your conscious belief.

Regardless of what you see, there is cause to everything that happens in your life. You don't know what it is, but many times there are patterns.

How much do our thoughts have an effect on our lives in terms of creating and influencing the circumstances? There is God's agenda and our opportunity to choose to go beyond our normal patterns of reaction and choose a higher reaction. Having a higher belief and thought is our ability to think and pray.

> *This is the bread of affliction that our forefathers ate in the land of Egypt.*

Our Sages of blessed memory have said, "At the time that Israel does the will of God, they are called children. And when they are not doing the will of God, they are called servants."[11]

These words are difficult to understand. When a person is not performing the will of God, shouldn't he be called wicked?

When a man believes with complete faith that the Holy One, blessed be He, is his Father, and that just as a parent has great pleasure in bestowing to his or her child, so too does our Father have pleasure when He bestows goodness on His people Israel, that frame of mind helps one become whole, making them ultimately grasp that they are not lacking anything—a totally trusting relationship regardless of the outcome. The relationship is whole, and there is nothing lacking. And when that person makes a request of God, e.g., that God should have compassion on His people, then with certainty God will fulfill that request.

This is the hint in the verse, "You will be whole with Hashem your God," as if to say that you will be whole and lacking nothing "when you will be with God."

However, when a person does not believe (that Hashem is our Father Who loves to give to His child), then that person is considered lacking because he is not *making it* the will of his Creator to bestow upon him good things.

This is hinted at by the phrase "bread of affliction" (bread of the poor). When Israel was in Egypt, they were in the aspect of "smallness." On this, our Sages of blessed memory have said, "Bread of affliction—the

---

11   *Bava Basra* 10a.

way of a poor person is to divide and partake of a slice, because the word *perusah* [slice in Hebrew] is the same expression as 'lacking.'"¹²

DRAWING FROM THE INFINITE SOURCE

הֶאָנֹכִי הָרִיתִי אֵת כָּל הָעָם הַזֶּה אִם אָנֹכִי יְלִדְתִּיהוּ כִּי תֹאמַר אֵלַי שָׂאֵהוּ בְחֵיקֶךָ כַּאֲשֶׁר יִשָּׂא הָאֹמֵן אֶת הַיֹּנֵק עַל הָאֲדָמָה אֲשֶׁר נִשְׁבַּעְתָּ לַאֲבֹתָיו.

Did I conceive this entire people, or did I give birth to it, that You say to me, "Carry them in your bosom, as a nurse carries a suckling, to the land that You swore to its fathers?"

Bamidbar 11:12

Here, the word "nurse" has the same root as *emunah*. What is the relation of nursing a child to faith?

אִם לֹא שִׁוִּיתִי וְדוֹמַמְתִּי נַפְשִׁי כְּגָמֻל עֲלֵי אִמּוֹ כַּגָּמֻל עָלַי נַפְשִׁי.

I swear that I stilled and silenced my soul, like a suckling child at his mother's side, like the suckling child is my soul.

Tehillim 132:2

The words of King David correlating the suckling child to the soul saying, "Just like a nursing child is satisfied after he has eaten and does not even think of worrying about when his next meal is coming from, so too is my soul. It has nothing to worry about."

When a child nurses, the milk comes as a result of his sucking. He draws it down, thereby causing more milk to be made for the next feeding. So too is *emunah* in relation to the ability to believe. The belief is the way that we draw down the abundance (*shefa*) from the Master

---

12 *Kedushas Levi*, Pesach Haggadah: *Bread of Affliction*. The idea is that you initiate, or rather realize, i.e., make real the relationship. How do you approach God? As a son to a father or as a servant to a master.

of the world. If there is no trust, there is no abundance; that's the way the system works! *Emunah* produces blessing.

Our Creator made us to be a vessel to receive the infinite. It's that simple. We will become a vessel, and there are only two ways to get there: we awaken and build ourselves from below, or we receive stimuli from above. We will move up the ladder either by self-motivation or by being kicked from behind, but move we will! God is an insistent King, and He will get His way. You will experience Infinity, and you will enjoy it!

CHAPTER FIVE

THE TORAH— THE BEST AND ONLY KOSHER THOUGHT DIET

Beloved are the People of Israel who were given a cherished vessel with which the world was created. An even greater endearment is that it was made known to them.

Pirkei Avos 3:18

NOW THAT WE HAVE discussed the power of our thoughts and our perceptions, we can easily commit to being connoisseurs of only the best thoughts and highest perceptions. So, what are these best and higher thoughts? What better place to go for the most unlimited thoughts and perceptions than the Unlimited Creative Intelligence Who revealed Himself to us at Mount Sinai and gave us the holy Torah?

Some of us might have preconceived notions and ideas about the revelation on Mount Sinai and what the Torah is. I kindly ask those of you who might have a previous perception to put those thoughts aside and venture with me to approach things from a different angle.

I always had the thought: "How could it be that I can go and buy a table lamp, and it comes with instructions, and yet we human beings, who are so much more complicated, did not come with instructions?" After traveling through Europe, the answer arrived when I came to

Jerusalem. Before deciding which kibbutz to visit, I was brought to a rabbinical school called a "yeshiva." There, I was introduced to the instruction manual of life, the Torah, which we received on Mount Sinai.

At Mount Sinai, somewhere between 2.5 to 3 million people had a simultaneous experience of the Infinite Creator, an event to which no other nation makes a claim. The revelation on Mount Sinai could have repaired mankind by imbuing us with the ultimate thoughts, thereby creating the greatest reality for all humanity. We were free from death and any outside, limited influence. We were tantamount to Adam and Chavah in the Garden of Eden before the original sin. However, a major setback occurred: the sin of the golden calf. In the scheme of things, we say that the incident of the golden calf was meant to be.[1] The result, however, made the path to completion a very long road. The bottom line is that within the Torah are the right thoughts, attitudes, and actions that will facilitate world repair.

There is not enough ink and paper that would scratch the surface to even begin to speak about the Torah and what was given to us by the Unlimited Creative Intelligence. It was given by the *Ein Sof* (unlimited), therefore it is *ein sof* (unlimited). But with the help of Heaven, I will try to cover a few ideas and themes.

ULTIMATE CLEANSE OF THE TREE OF KNOWLEDGE OF GOOD AND EVIL

I remember being in a junior high school assembly when a psychologist performed a simple demonstration. He had a glass bowl full of black liquid placed in a bigger glass bowl. He explained that the dark bowl represented our minds, and our minds are full of junk. The way to clear our minds was to fill it with purer thoughts. He then poured clear

---

1   *Avodah Zarah* 4b–5a.

water from a pitcher into the dark bowl. As the dark bowl overflowed to the bigger outer bowl, the dark bowl became clean. The simple demonstration clearly illustrated that an influx of clear, positive thoughts can flush out the dirty contents in our minds.

Adam and Chavah ate from the Tree of Knowledge of Good and Evil. What was this Tree of Knowledge? Was it pure evil? This "tree" was not called the "Tree of Knowledge of Evil," but, rather, "the Tree of Knowledge of Good *and* Evil"—a mixture that causes confusion. Simply put, before the sin, everything that was good was sweet, and whatever was bad was bitter—in a literal sense and in a spiritual sense. It was clear what to do and what to avoid.

After they ate, everything became confused, and from then on, not everything that is sweet is good for us and not everything that is bitter is bad for us, e.g., medicines. We are still affected by it until this day, and it was what can be called the "virus program of obscured perception."

For our topic of thoughts and ideas, we will explain the Tree of Knowledge of Good and Evil to be a mixture of limited-style thinking and unlimited-style thinking. Obviously, the limited thinking related to evil. We are confused and have difficulty distinguishing the thoughts that sabotage and limit us.

The mind is in need of a cleanse. The Torah is the cure.

Kosher Thought #1

Let's start with the first direct communication: "I am the Lord your God, Who brought you out of the land of Egypt." We are taught that besides the 2.5 to 3 million people that were there, all of our souls and any soul that would ever exist in the future were there. We all experienced this direct energy flow expressed in these words. With our theme of investing in the highest thoughts, this thought is the highest, the introduction to Infinity.

To put this first directive in other words:

- "Hello, I am the 'IS,'"[2]—the Unlimited Creative Intelligence. I am ungraspable; no one created Me. I have always existed.
- "Your God"—your "go to, your Source. There is nothing I cannot do."
- "Who brought you out of the land of Egypt."

Many commentators have questioned why it did not say, "Who created the heavens and the earth." Wouldn't that be a greater expression of introduction? "I am the One Who made all of this!" Why settle for "Who brought you out of Egypt"?

They explain that the Unlimited Creative Intelligence wanted to convey the idea that He is involved in our individual lives; "I am with you, and I interact with you." But more than that, the Hebrew word for Egypt is *Mitzrayim*, which the mystics explain is composed of two words: *meitzar yam*, the word "*meitzar*" meaning "constricted," and the word "*yam*" meaning sea/ocean. The idea of them together is "sea of constriction." The paradigm of Egypt is the impossible scenario. There was absolutely no way that we could have gotten out of Egypt were it not for God Who brought us out. Therefore, Egypt is the symbol of "the problem." So, to turn the first of the ten commandments into a thought-diet construct, we would say…[3]

> "I am the IS, your power Source,
> Who solves all your problems."

---

2   My expression for condensing His name of "was, is, and will be."
3   You might ask, "Why should there be problems in the first place?"

The answer is that we all became infected with constricted consciousness through the eating of the fruit of the Tree of Knowledge of Good and Evil.

That is cleansing element number one. The idea is to create the angel consciousness that we are going out of all of our self-imposed limitations every day, and the only thought that does that is "Infinity is involved in our lives," or, "I am connected to Infinity." The real expression with which we fulfill this thought is the recitation of: "Hear Israel, The Lord is our God, the Lord is One." This can be simplified to say: "The IS is our source. The IS is all there is."[4]

Kosher Thought #2

"Don't have any other gods before Me," which we translate as:

> *Don't go anywhere else for the solution to your problems.*

The idea is logically stated that if you believe in something else other than *ein sof* (unlimited), then you are believing in something limited. If you believe in limited, you get limited. If you believe in God and something else, then the universe echoes that. It allows you to rely on that finiteness, and good luck with all that.[5] If you look to finiteness for your solutions, then you get finiteness as your answer, as the prophet says, "They turn to empty cisterns for the solutions to their problems."

---

4   See *Sefer HaTanya*, chap. 47, where it explains that every day a person should see himself as if God brought him out of Egypt that day.
5   *Chovos Halevavos, Shaar Habitachon*, chap. 1.

Imagine your life fully operating with these two concepts in mind: "Go Infinite!" and "Stay away from finite."

> "I am connected to the Infinite Source!"

Here are a few basic ideas one needs to understand and integrate:

The Torah Is Eternal

Since the Torah is a code of how to connect the finite to the Infinite, it has to always have a relevance in the deepest level for our souls, right here and now. All the Chassidic masters and followers of the Baal Shem Tov expound the Torah based on this understanding. Every story and every directive have to connect us in some way to the here and now.

One way to see the eternal aspect of the Torah is to view the various individuals portrayed as archetypes or paradigms. The way they thought, spoke, and acted becomes a sort of "program." For example, Kayin and Hevel were of the two first archetype personalities. The Hebrew root of the name *Kayin* in Hebrew means "acquire." Chavah exclaimed, "I have a acquired a man with God." The idea of the name implies "I take in, give it to me," in essence, ego. Hevel, on the other hand, means vapor or air. His attitude was, "All things of this world are air and nothing." These two roles or patterns of existence are at two polar opposites: Selfishness on one side, and complete nullification on the other.

The truth is that they need to be balanced. One needs a sense of "I," as we are taught everyone is obligated to say, "For me, the world was created."[6] This does not mean the world was created for me with a sense of entitlement, but rather, as Rabbi Nachman explains, it

---

6   *Sanhedrin* 37a.

means to see what the world is lacking and pray for it and work to fix it. For the personality type of Hevel, one cannot say, "all is meaningless." Moshe our teacher, who was a reincarnation of Hevel, fixed this quality: Being the humblest man in the world, he understood that all is an illusion or air, but it has meaning—the meaning that God gives it, which is Torah and mitzvos.[7]

The same goes for the evil characters in the Torah as well. We see how they behaved, and we learn from them what not to do. Pharaoh is a great example. When things got unbearable for him during the ten plagues, he would exclaim, "God is just, I sinned." And then as soon as the plague was gone, he went right back into his old behavior. These patterns of behavior are potentially within us as well—aspects within our own souls that we must sweeten and elevate.

The *Sulam*, Rabbi Yehudah Leib Ashlag, writes in an article as follows:

> *When it really comes down to it, there is really only one soul. Only the body fashions for us the illusion of separation. That means, in a certain sense, we are all connected. Even with the great souls of the past! In the spiritual realm, there is no time or space. So, those holy souls are existing right here and now. My father-in-law, o.b.m., explained that within our individual soul is a "sliver" of everyone else's soul. So, when we align ourselves to some degree, to the deeds of those holy souls, we allow that energy and expression to manifest through us. So, in a micro-sense, when we conquer our evil traits, we are at that moment Yehoshua conquering the Land of Israel! When we come out of a rough predicament, we are the Jewish People leaving Egypt. When we repent and make amends of our past misdeeds, we are in a sense King David.*

---

7 Shem MiShmuel, Bamidbar, Parashas Korach.

Being that we are all one soul and all souls are included within each of us, we can connect to these paradigms, starting with our thoughts. We can do this by borrowing from a modern term used in technology: "program" or "application." Whenever we want to access those soul energies, we tune in by asking, "What were the thoughts the other person could possibly be having, but more so the beliefs?"[8] In this way, we allow ourselves to tune into that soul frequency and open ourselves up to that influence. When we align ourselves with those types of thoughts and desires, we are able to then be open to access and express our own unique soul frequency.

The Torah Is the Blueprint of Creation

With all the infinite depth of the Torah, when we look at it from an external viewpoint, the Torah basically consists of two things:

1. The basic storyline of a family that goes down to Egypt, becomes enslaved, is redeemed, and embarks on a journey to their homeland.
2. The 613 directives, called *mitzvos* in Hebrew, listed throughout the five books of Moshe.

In a deeper aspect, the Torah can be summed up in two concepts: exile and redemption, darkness and light. If you look at the storyline, it's the story of a family that went into exile where they became enslaved and were eventually redeemed and journeyed to their homeland. The 613 directives also have this aspect, as we will soon see. The idea being expressed as "from darkness, one can know light."[9]

---

8   Many times, Rabbi Nachman uses the word/expression *"bechinah,"* translated loosely as "aspect." When one's mind and action are aligned a certain way, they are in "the aspect of," the "formula of," or "in the program of," as if one is operating from that application or program.

9   *Tikkunei Zohar* 123b.

In an even deeper sense, the Torah is the blueprint of Creation. We have a teaching that God looked into the Torah and created the world.[10] However, the understanding of blueprint is not what we usually assume—that once we use the blueprint to build the structure, we then put it away. This blueprint, however, is a constant, dynamic expression. In the first chapter of *Bereishis*, God uttered ten utterances, and the world came into being. According to Kabbalistic tradition, it is still being willed into existence every moment.[11]

To understand this, we will explain the Torah and Creation using an analogy of a film projector, the film, and the screen. The projector is the light of God—the primordial will and life force of everything in Creation in its source form. The Torah is the film that delineates and constricts the light to form everything that is projected onto the screen. The screen is the world that we are experiencing. Everything that we experience in the world must originate from the film, which is the blueprint. Everything has its root in the blueprint/film. We always seek to trace an event or a thing back to the film.[12] Once we located it in the film and the source, we can know and appreciate its essence and, thereby, enhance its expression.

The Torah comes from the Creator. It is perfect and whole. Yet, why do we see so much "room for improvement" in what's being projected on the screen? The answer is that since the Torah is in this dynamic expression, it gives us the opportunity to be co-creators with God. "God looked into the Torah and created the world." "He gave us this precious gift in which the world was created." Why? For rectification and enhancement. A tree in the field can grow fruit. However, if the

---

10   *Zohar, Korach* 178a.
11   *Tanya, Shaar Yichud V'Emunah*, chap. 1, "Forever God Your word stands in the Heaven." The Baal Shem Tov said that those words are still being uttered, animating everything in existence.
12   E.g., our Sages ask, "Where is Haman alluded to in the Torah?" *Chullin* 139b.

tree is pruned, fertilized, and watered regularly, it can produce more and better fruit.[13]

The revelation on Mount Sinai is likened to a wedding. God is the groom, Israel is the bride, and the Torah is the contract. Since we accepted it, we are under contract. We accepted and must fulfill our obligations to such a degree that if the Torah is not learned and kept, the entire world would cease to exist. We are such dynamic "conduits" that if we do not fulfill the Torah, we block or contort the Divine light; the film or conduit for the Divine flow is obscured. If we fulfill it, then we allow that Divine light to flow into Creation.[14] In another sense, having received the Torah gives us a lot of power. The holy righteous people were able to manifest things through the creational force of the Torah.[15]

The Torah Is a Technology

Another way of looking is to say that the Torah is a very precious vessel in which the universe was and is presently being formed. God gave us this precious vessel, and an even greater expression of endearment is that He let us know about it. Not only must we deepen our appreciation for this special gift, but since it is a crafting tool, we must utilize it.

---

13 See *Midrash Tanchuma*, *Tazria* 5, where the wicked Turnusrufus asked Rabbi Akiva what is greater—something in which God makes or that which man makes? He was referring to the mitzvah of *bris milah*. Rabbi Akiva answered by presenting raw wheat stalks and an already-made cake, showing him that what man makes is better.
14 Mankind was always responsible for its actions, and the Torah always existed, but the goal was to have a people actualize it.
15 See Rabbi Akiva Tatz, *Worldmask*. *Yevamos* 121b brings a story of Rabbi Chaninah ben Dosa, who, when asked about the girl who fell into the well, explained that the father of the girl who built the well for the mitzvah of providing travelers' water will not suffer the loss. She emerged several hours later unharmed. This is because the righteous man facilitated a projection of the Torah in that way.

So, what is this utilization? Yes, an instruction manual for living a highly qualitative life, complete with moral values, but something much more: Attachment.

The Torah is a technology given to us by the Unlimited Creative Intelligence for the purpose of enlightening a path—a path for finite beings, i.e., us, to connect to the Infinite. If one could express the will of the Torah in one word, that word would be "attachment"—to be attached to the Infinite in a dynamic relationship.

To experience that attachment, there first has to be an experience of disconnect. Just as light cannot be fully appreciated if it is not contrasted by darkness, so too, part of the process of our existence is to experience disconnect in order to appreciate connection. Hence, this is why the main theme of the Torah is exile and redemption. As I stated above, we see the basic storyline being that of a family going into exile and coming out.

What is this connection? Judaism 101 teaches that the purpose of Creation is to bestow pleasure.[16] The Unlimited Creative Intelligence willed to bestow pleasure or goodness to another. That other is us, mankind. The nature of that pleasure, which God wants to bestow, is Himself. God loves His creation and only wants the absolute best for them. There is nothing better than Himself, since He is the Source of all pleasures imaginable and beyond. The pleasure, therefore, is not a physical pleasure but rather a spiritual one. God wishes to bestow Himself.

The obvious question is: if God wishes to bestow pleasure to another, why didn't He instantly create us already receiving this pleasure in

---

16   Rabbi Yitzchak Luria, the Arizal, *Eitz Chaim, Shaar Haklalim*, chap. 1. See Rabbi Yehudah Leib Ashlag's *Sulam*, Introduction to the *Zohar*, paragraph 6; Rabbi Aryeh Kaplan, *Inner Space*, p. 9; *Zohar, Parashas Bo* 142, which brings another expression: "To reveal His Godliness to another."

the first place? Moreover, our experience of this world is one full of tremendous suffering and, outwardly, it doesn't seem to be fitting that idea of bestowal of pleasure at all.

The truth is that in our primordial, unified soul form, once upon a time, we were receiving that pleasure. But because we were made in the image and likeness of God, we couldn't take that infinite pleasure without giving something back or earning it. God's image, so to speak, is only interested in giving. He does not need to receive from anyone. So, we too have that form within us in that we also have a will to bestow and not just receive.

Here, we reach the deep concept called in our tradition the "bread of shame." Imagine a poor person who receives his daily bread from a wealthy person. Because of his embarrassment, the poor person cannot look into the face of the one giving it to him.

So, this one universal soul, so to speak, turned to The Infinite Source and said, "I don't want this pleasure anymore."

God asked, "Why?"

"Because it's too embarrassing for me to just receive and not do anything to earn it."

So, God said, "Fine. I'll make a world in which I will hide Myself and put you down in there. You will have the opportunity, through your free choice, to earn the pleasure that I wish to give you."

Thus, God made a world, a Garden, Adam, and Chavah, and gave them one opportunity, saying, "Don't eat from the Tree of Knowledge of Good and Evil." They ate from the tree, and as a result of their exercise of their free choice, here we are having to combat the forces of negative influence to earn the perfection that God wishes to bestow upon us.

Therefore, as part of the consequence and rectification process, Adam and Chavah were expelled from the Garden and sent into exile. And here we are, all of us, the descendants of Adam and Chavah, and we're still infected with this "knowledge of good and evil," or what I would call a "consciousness of confusion and limitation." Rabbi Nachman expresses it by saying we ate from the tainted grain and went crazy.[17]

FORMS OF EXILE

There are many forms of exile in our tradition: the exile of the soul within the body; the exile of the mind; the physical exile from one's homeland; the exile of Torah; and the exile of prayer.

The Exile of the Soul within the Body

Our soul comes from a very high place in the spiritual realm. We were bathing in the light of God and enjoying blissful existence. The *Zohar* brings a parable of a king who went for a stroll with one of his servants. The stroll led them to walk up a high tower with a staircase winding above, higher and higher. Upon the wall of every step of this tower was mounted a portrait of someone different with each step. As the king and the servant are ascending, they suddenly stop, and the king directs his servant to one of the portraits asking him what his opinion is of this portrait. The servant does not answer, whereas the king responds that this portrait is who the servant is going to be in the world below. The servant shockingly replies, "No way! I like it here! I don't want to be that person!" The king then explains to the servant that in the great scheme of things, it's for the absolute best. The lesson is that the King, Who is our Creator, explains it to the servant, who is the soul, and he finally agrees to descend into a body. Hence, the soul goes from its beautiful place above to be in a coarse body with all its deviant influences.

---

17   See Rabbi Nachman's story about the tainted grain.

The Exile of the Mind

This could also be called an exile of identity. In the beginning of *Sefer Shemos*, a peculiar theme is taking place. At the onset of the Egyptian exile, there are no real names mentioned. The two midwives we know are Yocheved and Miriam, yet they are referred to as Shifrah and Puah because of how they behave with the newborn infants. In chapter two, it states, "A man from the house of Levi went and took a daughter of Levi." Here also we know that it is referring to Amram, the leader of the Jewish People, and Yocheved, his wife, who he reunited with. No names. She gave birth to a son with no name. His sister followed to see what would be. The daughter of Pharaoh went down to the river, etc. Not until after the boy was weaned and brought to the daughter of Pharaoh was he given the name Moshe.

The Egyptian exile is the paradigm of all exiles. What happens there serves as a root for all the other exiles that will follow. The fact that there were no names mentioned indicates no identity. No name. We can't express ourselves until we know who we are.

Another form of the exile of the mind is our inability to self-actualize and realize our potential.[18] Also, the inability of the mind to connect with the heart and charge it to feel the right feeling at the right time. For example: There is a commandment to love every Jewish soul. We say this every morning before we pray, "I now accept upon myself the positive commandment to love every Jew like myself." One can say this easily, but one might ask themselves how much they really feel it. Is there any resistance? Even the slightest bit? We know what the right thing to do is, but there is a blockage, to some degree. This is a form of exile of the mind. It just doesn't work right.

---

18 *Baal Shem Tov on the Torah, Shemos* 20:1. See also *Toldos Yaakov Yosef, Shemos* 38:8.

Physical Exile from One's Homeland

This should be obvious. Wherever we find our home, we get used to that area and a certain way of life. If anyone has ever traveled and stayed away from home for any length of time, they experience a certain vulnerability, especially if they get lost trying to find the hotel or airport or the like. How happy they are when they return home.

The Exile of the Torah

Rabbi Moshe Chaim Luzzatto mentions this in his work *Maamar on Redemption* that the Torah is in exile. My rabbi and father-in-law, Rabbi Shabtai Teicher, explained it to me that each of the many sects of Orthodox Judaism claim that they have the whole Torah. They have part, but not all. The Torah is whole, but it gives the impression that it's fragmented. They might have the whole book, but usually they are emphasizing one thing over another. For example, one might experience some groups who put mitzvos between man and God over mitzvos between man and man. Another sect might do the opposite. Many teachings passed down from generation to generation, some ideas are not emphasized, asserted and taught enough. For example, "Loving your neighbor as yourself." When I taught a group of adults that according to the Arizal we must say this every morning, one person remarked, "Why weren't we taught this in schools?"

Exile of Prayer

Rabbi Nachman mentions this in his magnum opus, *Likutei Moharan*, that prayer is now in exile. Let's face it, how many people do it by rote? He writes that it is "something that stands in the height of heights, and people step on it and cheapen it, wanting to get it over with."[19] A person can actually talk with the ultimate Source Who desires to have a relationship with us, and yet they focus on what's for lunch? Sad.

---

19 *Likutei Moharan* II 1:8.

The modern way to escape this way of thinking is to realize that the Torah itself was only given 3,334 years ago. It is called "The Tree of Life."

The Torah is a technology and a remedy: a technology for the soul to work itself through its limited and confused style of thinking, which we call the Tree of Knowledge of Good and Evil, developing itself to becoming the ultimate vessel to receive the Infinite light. However, this final stage of total connection to the Unlimited Creative Intelligence, Whom we call God, requires the necessary ingredient called free will. We have to want and choose to be in a relationship with the Creator.

The Torah is the way to work through the issue of the "bread of shame." In order to be able to reward us for our choices, we have to face a real challenge; there has to be serious competition in our choosing, which has the ability to eclipse the light and love of God through things like physical pleasures and distractions. The illusion of "other than God," i.e., this material world and all its pleasures, presents itself as so real that we get caught up in it. The Kabbalah calls it the husks, or *kelipos*—something external and non-essential, yet leading us to believe that it is essential or important. The Torah provides the navigation to discern between good and evil and work our own way out of the mess in which we find ourselves.

PACKAGING THE TECHNOLOGY

If you were the *Ein Sof* and wanted to give mankind the ultimate instructions on its mission and purpose in life, how would you do it? It would have to be something that would fit the tastes and visions of everyone young, old, bright, less-bright, etc. Only the Infinite Creator can create a manual of life that a three-year-old child can enjoy and an eighty-year-old genius can revel in all his days. On the surface, it has stories that awaken the children, and yet it contains the deepest mystery formulas for geniuses. Within it is the code of the universe and the ultimate thought diet.

TORAH IS LIKENED TO WATER

Everyone who's thirsty, go to the water.

Yeshayahu 55:1

From this verse, the Torah is compared to water.[20] There are several ideas expressed relating the nature of the comparison. Some write, "Just as water always flows to the lowest place, so too does the Torah flow only to those who are humble in nature."[21] Another idea is: "Just as water is life for the world, so too the Torah is life to the body."[22] The one idea I wish to focus on is from the *Midrash Tanchuma*,[23] which indicates that those who study Torah are as those who are watering the seeds. Perhaps we can say that just as water causes whatever seeds planted in the ground to grow, so too does the Torah exponentially take our thoughts and bring out whatever it is we are thinking. Given that we are already in the form of God, creating and manifesting, the Torah has potential to bring our thoughts to another level. An amazing thing about the Torah is that it is "user-friendly," which means that it teaches and guides one to think the right thoughts to manifest the absolute best. The Creator is patient in our development toward maturity, so He understands that since we are coming from a place of limited thoughts, He will not allow a certain amount of destruction

---

20   *Rashi* ad loc.
21   *Derech Chaim* 6:6:16.
22   *Sifri, Devarim* 48:5.
23   *Midrash Tanchuma, Bereishis* 1:16: It is because of the reward given to those who devote themselves to the Torah that Yeshayah declared: "Happy are you that sow beside all waters, that send forth freely the feet of the ox and the ass" (*Yeshayahu* 32:20). The words "that sow beside all waters" refer to those who devote themselves to the study of the Torah, which is compared to water, as it is said: "Everyone that is thirsty, come for water" (ibid., 55:1); the word ox alludes to the Mashiach of the House of Yosef (a descendant of the house of Yosef will precede the coming of the Davidic Mashiach). Cf. *Sukkah* 52a, who is compared to an ox; and the ass refers to the Mashiach of the House of David, for it is said of him: "Lowly and riding upon an ass" (*Zecharyah* 9:9).

to take place. In essence, if one wishes to damage his or her soul with the wrong thought, word, or action, He will not allow that blemish to reach its full manifestation.[24]

THE INNER CONCEPT OF "MITZVOS"

If you look in the Hebrew dictionary, the word *tzeves* literally means to connect. So, when we say there are 613 "commandments" in the Torah, the word *commandment* is not exact. It really means "connections." Hence, there are 613 connections.

The holy *Zohar* describes mitzvos in two terms of *etin* (עטין) and *pikudin* (פיקודין), which mean "advice" and "deposit,"[25] respectively. How do we understand these definitions?

The truth of the matter is that in each of these very dynamic actions called "mitzvos," there are two functions. One is the actual performance of the directive, which is called "advice." The other is that a mitzvah has a "pocket" or a "deposit" of infinite energy contained within the action, the idea being that one cannot access the light until one performs the action first.[26]

This is why so many people who take a chance and actually observe Shabbos with all its rules, or will keep the kosher laws with all its guidelines, after a while will tend to feel different. For many, this feeling cannot be put into words. To observe as an outsider and exclaim, "I see no light in this" is true, just like you cannot go to a yoga, Pilates, or Tai Chi workout, observe the people involved all performing the moves while you sit and drink your latte and exclaim after the class, 'Wow, what a great workout." **So too, you will not taste the light until you do it**. Within these "actions of connections," we gain the access to the light. So, the children of Israel understood this at Mount Sinai when they

---

24   Arizal, *Shaar Higilgulim* (Gates of Reincarnation).
25   Actually, it is the word for "commandments" in Aramaic.
26   See the *Sulam*, prologue to the book of *Zohar*, paragraph 1.

exclaimed, "We will do and we will hear." In order to be in that connection, one must perform the act.[27] We are taught that at the time when the Jewish People said, "We will do and we will hear," the angels in Heaven got upset and claimed, "Who told them our secret?" The secret they were hinting to was that one must perform the deed first to access the light.

Kabbalistic tradition teaches that the 613 "commandments," or what we should really call connections, correspond to the parts of the body. That is, we have 248 positive directives that correspond to the 248 limbs of the body, and the 365 negative directives correspond to the 365 sinews. When one performs a mitzvah, they facilitate life-force energy to that part of the body. When one transgresses a negative commandment, they block the flow and vitality to that sinew. So, if we would view the Torah and mitzvos as a technology of the soul, it would make perfect sense; since the purpose of the Torah is attachment, i.e., for us to have a relationship with the Infinite, then the degree that one is in alignment with the directives contained therein will be the degree of their attachment.

WE ARE ALL INCLUDED IN THE TORAH

Everyone has a portion in the Torah. There were 600,000 soul roots that stood on Mount Sinai when the Torah was given. All of us today are branches of those root souls. We are taught that there are 600,000 letters in the Torah, and each root soul is expressed through one of those letters. One needs to do his own exploration to discover himself within the Torah. One should begin an exploration and discover what intrigues and tickles them. There are so many areas one can delve into—from practical Jewish law to the most esoteric wisdom. We are taught that a person should learn what his heart desires. Some souls

---

27   Rabbi Yehuda Leib Ashlag's *Sulam*, on his explanation of fourteen mitzvos, *Zohar* 1:242.

are more attracted to Jewish law, some like Talmud, some like Midrash, *Zohar*, or Kabbalah. Make a daily routine to swim in it and breathe in it. Allow the light of it to elevate you and your thinking. Seek out a teacher in the area you are most interested in and don't let go.

And give us please our portion in Your Torah.
Shabbos Tefillos

Rabbi Nachman writes that if someone wants to develop a deep love connection to the Torah, he must be very careful not to speak badly about another.

The reason is that since there are 600,000 letters in the Torah, corresponding the 600,000 root souls, if there is one letter of the Torah scroll besmirched or missing, the entire Torah scroll is invalid. Since every Jew is an expression of one of those letters, once someone, God forbid, would speak badly about someone, they would be blemishing for themselves that letter of the Torah. They have blemished their own cosmic Torah scroll and therefore will become disconnected and lose access to their own portion of Torah.

We pray three times a day, and on the Shabbos and the holidays, we say, "Give us our portion in Your Torah." It must be pointed out that the prayer is written in the plural, as with most prayers; we must yearn not only for our own portion and connection but for everyone else's as well. Imagine right now yearning for your neighbor and friend to connect and express their unique portion in the Torah. Right now, put yourself in a place such that you need all the people to access their portion in the Torah as if it's your oxygen!

> *"I can hardly wait to experience the unique Torah that my holy brothers and sisters have to teach me."*

Thinking people agree that, to some extent, our beliefs create our reality. If you believe you are weak, you will become weak. If you believe that you can go beyond, who is to tell you where the limit is? The truth is that only God can tell you, but for sure you shouldn't tell yourself. We all might have heard about the elephants in India who remain in place only because of the band tied around their back leg. When they were young, the actual band was tied to a post to prevent them from wandering. Once they became accustomed to staying put because of the positioned band, they grew up with the same habit—once the band was there, they could not move. The same is true with certain flies in a jar; the baby eagle raised among chickens that began pecking like a chicken, not thinking it could fly, etc. We can use these examples to examine where in our lives we might be limiting ourselves.

If our beliefs create our reality, then wouldn't it make sense to only infuse our minds with the thoughts of the Torah?

All the parts of the Torah are vital. No part can be belittled or overlooked. However, the inner parts of the Torah are what lead us more directly to expand beyond our limited, self-taught (or taught by others) beliefs.

Imagine getting a gift from the cosmos. This gift, if you would approach it, would manifest all your thoughts. If you were not on the right level of maturity, it would be quite dangerous. An external fear would bring about such a manifestation, God forbid. Thank God, the Torah is user-friendly in that there is oversight of the Creator Who is extremely patient with us in our development. However, we do have to make strides to develop our thinking.

Another key word that the Torah is centered upon is *emunah*, meaning faith. However, the translation of "faith" for some of us implies an almost passive type of attitude. I now understand this *emunah* to be utilized as "the power of belief"—to integrate the idea so deeply with in oneself that they resonate and vibrate with that idea. What an angel! What a reality!

In addition to imbuing the highest ideas and beliefs into our system, our connection and learning of the Torah enables all of our prayers and requests to be answered.[28]

---

28   Rabbi Nachman, *Likutei Moharan* 1:1. Imagine making a prayer and, boom, it happens. Wouldn't that be nice?

CHAPTER SIX
QUANTUM THINKING

Think good, and it will be good.

Tzemach Tzedek

THERE IS A CONCEPT in the world called the quantum leap. Usually, this refers to atoms and subatomic particles and how they interact with one another and travel. One mysterious wonder is that when one subatomic particle, called an electron, will travel to another part of the universe for whatever reason, it happens to instantly appear in its destination without a traceable path of travel. This is quite bizarre and still baffles many scientists, since in our known and observable universe, we can always trace a trajectory or path. But here, the electron will just disappear from its place and suddenly appear in another.

I would like to borrow the terminology of the quantum leap for our topic of the thoughts and feelings in which we engage in.

Let us revert to the earlier example of the tuning forks. If I have a tuning fork that resonates an "A" sound, it will only resonate or be resonated by something of the same frequency or vibration. In order to have a certain desired effect or experience in our lives, we have to first have the resonance or feeling tone before we can have that experience! We must feel what it feels like to have that livelihood, health, prosperity, success, fulfillment, etc., before we will have the actual experience.

This is what I call the "*Az Zone.*"

Let us return to what I mentioned in chapter four concerning the miracle of the parting of the Red Sea. The very first word that Moshe sang after the miracle was the word "*az.*" The holy Berditchever Rebbe, Rabbi Levi Yitzchak, gave an incredible explanation of this word "*az,*" which translates into English as "then." "Then, Moshe and the children of Israel sang the song…" This word "then" in the Hebrew word "*az*" is used to denote the future. It means, "then we will sing." But Moshe and the children of Israel sang the song *after* the event. How do we understand this? The Berditchever Rebbe explains that the song that they sang after the miracle was because of the power of trust that one person had *before* the miracle happened. His name was Nachshon ben Aminadav. As brought down in our oral tradition, he was the first to jump in the sea, even before it split. Nachshon had the energy and vibration as if the miracle had already begun. He truly was in the state that engendered the miracle to occur. Hence, Moshe had to begin the song with the energy of *az*, since it was this type of energy and attitude that triggered the sea to split.

The point is that one must use his power of belief to envision his situation and circumstances as if the emancipation or deliverance has already happened. He must utilize the power of "*Az*" in his daily living and project his mind to be in the realm of ultimate connection before the situation he is yearning for unfolds. This is truly the leap of faith—the quantum leap.

> *I will sing to God, for He has already bestowed His goodness upon me.*
>
> Tehillim 13:6

One idea that can help us is to know that in the spiritual world, there is no time. So, in a sense, everything that will happen has already happened or is happening right now; we just can't see it. It is meant to be that way in order for us to awaken and create within ourselves that feeling tone to produce the quantum leap of faith. In the spiritual realm, there is infinite pleasure being bestowed at all times. We can create a space even for a moment to attempt to tune into it. To utilize the rule of the Baal Shem Tov, "Wherever your thoughts are, that's where you are."

IMAGERY AND VISUALIZATION

A major part of utilizing our thoughts, besides using words and ideas, is also utilizing the power of imagery and visualization. Forming things in our minds has been a practice in many disciplines the world over. One example can be seen from an experiment where they took basketball players and divided them into two groups. One group actually did the physical practicing while the other half only visualized themselves practicing free throws. The group that merely visualized made a greater improvement compared to the group that practiced for half an hour every day.[1]

The power of forming in your mind has been one of the tools used in the Mussar Movement, initiated by Rabbi Yisrael Salanter. He would instruct his students to use the power of imagery to work on developing a character trait. A student would practice in his mind a certain behavior he wanted to change in anticipation of actually altering that behavior. Using this form of imagery is useful, but the ultimate place to reach is the feelings, or as I described earlier, the feeling tones. One has to believe it to produce the vibrational energy needed to attract the experience.[2]

I use this rule in my prayer and meditation. For example, I try and imagine what it would feel like for the world to be redeemed at this

---

1 Dr. Blaslotto study on visualization at the University of Chicago in 1996.
2 See also *Chayei Moharan* about Rabbi Nachman of Breslov, p. 516, on the topic of the righteous in the future world expressing, "This is the God we hoped for…" expressing the idea of tasting the connection to God of the future world while being in the present world.

moment. With every blessing that I say, I make an effort to realize that the *Ein Sof* is the Source of everything, that the Mashiach has already come, and that the eyes and hearts of humanity are now opened to have a direct relationship with the Unlimited. This is indicated by the fact that the blessings are written in present tense: "Blessed are You, God, Who heals the sick"; "Blessed are You, God, Redeemer of Israel." Could this be what the writers of the prayer book had in mind when they composed the prayer book? That these words would be used as a meditation of sorts for visualizing a fixed world? After all, why think small?

Remember: you have to feel the feelings first before you experience the reality.

I now present a list of basic ideas for the reader to dabble with. These ideas presented below have to make sense and resonate in order to create a more powerful angel/force for the full expression. Some call these affirmations, but affirmations work only when we believe them with conviction.

Note: The rest of the chapter is a list of dynamic thoughts that I use on a consistent basis from time to time to get me into a higher state. If these don't work for the reader, then I encourage you to find your own "power thoughts."

CREATING ANGELS—LEVEL ONE

Our first two rules:

1. I am the Lord your God, Who brought you out of Egypt.

    Don't forget rule number one: "I am the Lord your God, Who brought you out of Egypt." In our terminology: "I am your Unlimited Source, Who solves all of your problems."

    Sefer Tanya, chapter 47, writes that when one says "*Shema Yisrael*," a person has to view things as if that day God is bringing them out of Egypt. How is that so? One has to actualize that moment, seeing oneself as totally free of all obstacles that block one from expressing one's true soul-self.

So rule number one is "I am your problem solver." We need to combine this rule with rule number two.

2. Don't have any other gods before Me.

Rule number two: "Don't have any other gods before Me" means don't go elsewhere for the solutions to your problems. See the first chapter of the Gate of Trust in *Chovos Halevevos* by Ibn Paquda, who states that if one puts one's trust in something other than the Almighty Infinite Source, then measure for measure, the Source leaves that person to that other power (i.e., don't go after the empty cistern), and good luck with that!

THE FOREFATHERS

"What were the actions of the forefathers so that they were so close to the *Ein Sof*/Unlimited?"[3] "When will my deeds reach their deeds?"[4]

Step One: What were the thoughts of our forefathers (Avraham, Yitzchak, and Yaakov) that warranted that the Creator of the universe would connect with them, love them so much, and come to them, telling them, "You are it! Forever!"?

Although the connection to the *Ein Sof* of the forefathers was beyond what we can imagine, we can still put ourselves in the state of "as if we can imagine." Just to ask the question brings focus and motivation for the mind to extend toward that place.

So many times, when I say the first blessing in the silent prayer, I stop for a brief moment, just after the point that we say, "God of Avraham,

---

3   Rabbi Yitzchak Shir, *Emek Hahavanah B'Torah U'B'Chazal*, chap. 1.
4   Ibid., quoting *Tanna D'bei Eliyahu* 4: "Therefore I said that everyone from Israel is obligated to say, 'When will my deeds...'" Also quoting Rabbi Moshe Chaim Luzzatto, *Derech Eitz Chaim*: "Thinking in this way [i.e., asking ourselves, 'When will my deeds...'] is the most powerful thought against the negative self-sabotaging forces of our evil inclination."

God of Yitzchak, and God of Yaakov," and I ask in my mind, "What were the thoughts of our forefathers that they had such a connection to the Infinite? What were their perceptions? Their aspirations? Their dreams? Their desires? Their goals? Their passions? Their words and their deeds?"

Step Two: "When will my thoughts, speech, and deeds reach toward the level of the thoughts, speech, and deeds of the forefathers?" Just meditate on that and imagine as if your thoughts, speech, and deeds already have reached that point.[5]

When we say the blessing three times a day in the daily prayer book, "Blessed are You, God, shield of Avraham," we are recognizing and increasing that awareness of who we are. Avraham was a revolutionary who brought total awareness of the Oneness of God and the love He has for His creations. Avraham always sought this elevation and rectification, going against the entire generation of idolaters. "One was Avraham," the prophet Yechezkel said.[6] He looked upon himself, thinking, "I am the only one who can bring out this message." And he allowed no one to be an obstacle and paid no attention to anyone ridiculing him. Rabbi Nachman says: So too if someone wishes to enter into the service of God, he cannot do so without this formula called "one was Avraham," to consider themselves as the only one in the world with a unique message and expression. When we say this blessing, we are realizing that we are from Avraham and his creed.[7]

---

5   Our tradition, however, teaches that our deeds will never actually reach the level of their deeds. Hard as it sounds coming from a book about breaking out of our limited beliefs, I choose to accept this tradition, and yet still strive to get as close as possible. It's like one of those geometric curves that gets ever closer and closer to naught but never touches it. I can live with that.
6   33:24.
7   See the *hashmatos* (omissions) of *Likutei Moharan*, found in between volumes 1 and 2.

> *Always remember, God is always with you.*
> Rabbi Eliezer's last words to his son Rabbi Yisrael, the Baal Shem Tov

The Israelites saw the ten plagues in Egypt and more at the parting of the Red Sea. Yet, not too long after their departure, they entertained the idea of "Is God with us or not?" Immediately thereafter, Israel waged war with Amalek. The word *Amalek* in Hebrew has the same numerical value as the Hebrew word *safek* (doubt). When we contemplate ideas of doubt, they result in a manifestation of that doubt. The ultimate thought to combat that doubt is to know with absolute conviction: **"God is with us!"** If we think anything less than that, then "zap," that is what we are creating.

"God is with me," no matter what. "The *Ein Sof* is with me." Or,

> *"Is there a place where the Infiniteness of God ends, and we begin?"*

THE SIX CONSTANT MITZVOS

The following are known to all as the Six Constant Mitzvos that one is meant to contemplate at all times with one's mind. Below, I have rendered them according to our special terminology:

1. I believe in the Infinite IS-ness, Who creates and guides all reality and experience in all existence.
2. I believe that there is no other power or source other than the Infinite IS-ness.
3. The Infinite IS-ness is One. Hear Israel, the Lord Who is our God, the Lord is One. The Creator Who creates and guides all things in existence has no partner in Creation. He rules over everything and all there is.

4. To be in a state of absolute love with the IS-ness.
5. To be in a state of awe, realizing the Infinite IS-ness is beyond all contemplation. No thought can contain Him. No one made the Is. He has always existed and will always exist. He alone is absolute existence.
6. I will not allow my heart or my eyes to deviate from my sincere relationship, appreciation, and dedication with my Creator. I have everything and there is no need to look upon and compare what I have with what others possess.

MORE IDEAS TO CONTEMPLATE

The following are more ideas that, if one thinks about them, can really help to set one's mind in the right place.

"I am His trusted servant."

Make believe that God whispers in your ear, "You are My trusted servant. You always have been and always will be."

How would that make you feel? "Blessed are You, God, Who has made us all to be Your perfect servants today."

All of our souls were at Mount Sinai, and we all accepted to be servants of the All There Is. Can we now have the chutzpah to think we know what it feels like, as if we have made it to that place?

"Wow! I had no idea that God could be this good!"

What would it feel like to say this with absolute meaning, feeling, sincerity, enthusiasm, consistency, excitement, seriousness, and dedication?

We can look upon the suffering of the world and feel like we can't even think such a thought as the above, but try to put that aside for now and know that everything God is doing is building us to be vessels to reflect His infinite light. In the end, we will be shown in some incredible way that all that suffering, no matter how hard, was for our ultimate good. Imagine being in the future and being shown how the Infinite has flipped all the suffering into joy. What would that feel like? Try to feel the feeling even if just for a moment. Put yourself in your mind as if you and all of Creation are actually there.

"Thank You, God, for making it so easy to say, 'My life for You!'"

This is a big one to swallow, but we would like to be in the state where we hold nothing back from God, even for a moment. The *Tzettel Katan*, "*The Little Text*" by the *Noam Elimelech*, states that one must be willing to sacrifice his life for the sanctification of the name of God should the occasion arise. There are three directives for which we have to give up our lives rather than transgress them: idolatry, murder, and forbidden relations. Imagine that you are being brought in front of an idol and told to bow down to it or die. What an opportunity to show your devotion to God!

In other words, while one is waiting in line at the post office or grocery store, instead of looking at the phone, one could contemplate the mitzvah of giving over one's life for the sanctification of the Holy One. The question we can ask ourselves in the face of such an experience is, "What perceptions, what contemplations, what attitudes, and what feelings must one be contemplating to fulfill this mitzvah with love?"

This is actually one of the special meditations from the teachings of the Kabbalah when we say *k'rias Shema* and we get to the words "with love" in the first blessing of the silent prayer. Basically, it comes out a minimum of five times a day where we have the opportunity to practice creating this feeling tone: twice when we say *Shema* and three times when we are in the silent *Amidah* and say the words, "For the sake of His name with love." The quantum thought is to imagine you already having the perception. Imagine you already have the feeling tone. Even if a person has never experienced such a thing, a person can make-believe and create it within himself to some degree. Imagine that you have that much love and faith in the Creator that you can say this line with great love and joy and that you are totally, happily willing to give up your soul for The Oneness.

"I can hardly wait to see how this change of plans will enhance my life in a greater way!"

This one you need to always have on you—when you get a flat tire on the road, when your oven explodes, or when there is no hot water in your house. First, however, one has to habituate himself to saying, "Thank You, God!"

> When confronted by thoughts of fear, use this: "These thoughts of fear are nothing more than a habit. They are simply not me."

> When encountering thoughts of doubt, God forbid, use this: "These thoughts of doubt are nothing more than a habit. They are simply not me. What an easy habit to break!"

> Remember the people of Amalek, who are the *gematria* of the word *doubt* in Hebrew, and feel the feelings of: "I am finally doubt-free!"

> "There is nothing else other than God. He is all there is."[8]

> "It's almost unbelievable how God has turned all of us into His perfect servants (trusting Him totally), and we are all giving Him a total of one-hundred percent *nachas* (gratification)."

> "Wow! I had no idea that God was that close to us!"

---

8   See *Nefesh Hachaim, Shaar* 3, "*Ein Od Milvado.*"

"Oh yes! It is quite possible that God could be with us in that way with such overwhelming love all the time."[9]

"Wow! I had no idea God could be that loving! That kind! That compassionate!"

"I can hardly wait to see the life-enhancing experiences that God is going to bring to me today!"

"When will I merit that the spirit of the All There IS will rest on me? (Baal Shem Tov)

"This is amazing that I am witnessing in the most unbelievable way that God is removing the foreskins from all of our hearts and bringing us so close to Him."

I ask God "Why? Why are You doing all of this? To be giving so much good?" And He answers me and says, "That's just Who I am. I will be what I will be. Always with you."

"I got it! We got it!" The acceptance of the Kingdom of Heaven means we realize that there is nothing else other than God, and to accept it with full joy when we recite, "Hear Israel, the Lord is God, the Lord is One." Feel the feelings with the thoughts resounding in your mind, "I got it! We got it!"

This is a next-world thought

God wants to only give you infinite pleasure. "I have finally reached the point of becoming that vessel capable of receiving infinite pleasure in the right way. I am now receiving on the condition that I am giving

---

9   The *Leshem* writes in *Sefer Hade'ah* (*chelek* 8, *drush* 2, *anaf* 4, *siman* 6) that this is the ultimate *tikkun* (rectification).

through my receiving. The condition is that I only want for there to be the full expression of The Infinite Oneness. Yes! I have finally become that vessel for God to express His Infiniteness." Now is the part where you jump up and down fifty times, declaring, "Only for Your Glory, God, I wouldn't want it any other way. I will receive this great goodness only on the condition that You alone are glorified!"

> "There is nothing God cannot do by means of me, by means of us."

> "To forgive anyone, yes, I have that power. I now declare my right to that power—the power of forgiveness and letting go."

> "Thank You, God, for this cherished time to contemplate God-like thoughts."

> "There is a place where a person can accept even this event (whatever it might be) lovingly." *Do you believe that? How much?*

> "'Great is Your faith in me!' God is banking on me."

Every morning upon awakening, we say *Modeh Ani*, thanking God that He has returned our souls into our bodies with love. He has invested in us and has great faith in us. The issue is, do we have faith in ourselves?[10]

Picture now if you were giving a pitch before the richest, most successful person in the world for your idea to change the world, and he decides to invest in you because he sees something in you. Now, you are the children of the Omnipresent, and He is banking on you to overcome any obstacle and live your life's purpose with joy.

---

10   Rabbi Nachman, *Sichos HaRan* 140; Rav Tzadok Hakohen of Lublin, *Tzidkas Hatzaddik* 154.

"Thank You, God, for giving me absolute clarity in knowing and connecting with my mission!"

"All of my bones say, 'God, Who is like You!'" (*Tehillim* 35:10). In his classic work, *Nesivos Shalom*, the Slonimer Rebbe explains that there are three levels of belief and trust in God.[11] There is the level of faith and trust of the mind. A person can believe in the Almighty from an intellectual perspective, but his heart is not a hundred percent there. A deeper faith is one who believes intellectually and it even penetrates to the heart, where the person actually feels from an emotional perspective. But the deepest level is the believing from the limbs, to the degree that the thickest aspect of the person's body, i.e., the most solid place, trusts in the Almighty. This verse from *Tehillim* is actually written in the *Nishmas* prayer that we say every Shabbos. Why would it be there if we were not able to actualize this state of being?

Now you can contemplate:

"Thank You, God, that my whole mind can recognize that You are my Source. Thank You, God, that all my heart can know that You are my Source. Thank You, God, that all my bones can trust in You totally, that You are my Source."

Think of a kindness that God has and is doing for you, and repeat the words several times with energy and excitement:

> *Who is like You, God, Who is like You?*

"I am now allowing infinity to manifest its infiniteness by means of me."

Know that you were created for a purpose. When you are feeling that you have no purpose and don't know what to do with yourself, think this thought with conviction. Remember, you don't have to know

---

11   Slonimer Rebbe, *Nesivos Shalom*, *Parashas Vayeishev, Beshalach*.

what that expression or manifestation is. Just sit with the feeling tone for a while.

"God I am in awe of You! I love You!"

"I cannot stand the thought of being separated from You!"
Can you dare attempt to say this any time of the day?

"I'm going to sing and laugh about this!"

When you are in a situation that seems like you're stuck, try to put yourself in a joyous state and say this, "Remember, when they crossed the sea? They had the attitude that they will sing—holy chutzpah!"

**"Baruch/Blessed are You, God...,"
really translates as, "God, You are the Source."**

There is much depth to the word *"baruch"* that we literally translate as "blessed." One idea expressed from the book *Shaarei Orah* by Rabbi Yosef Gikatilla[12] is that it is associated with the word *bereichah*, in Hebrew meaning a pool, as in the source of water. When we say the word *"baruch"* in the beginning of a blessing, in essence we are acknowledging the Source, the source being the *Ein Sof*. In essence, we are saying, "You are our Source, God."

Blessings are hooking us into the zone of realizing we are not the source and that it is God. In a way, when we say a blessing, we are rejoicing in our dependency and our vulnerability, and we are in the best of hands.

> *"I can joyfully embrace my vulnerability!"*

---

12   *Shaar* 1.

"Who says the love that is in your heart is yours for you to keep?" This thought assumes that you already have so much love in your heart. The obvious implication of this is to go give it out.

> *Everything God does is for the good.*
> Rabbi Akiva[13]

The God of Hosts is with us…Right now, I take this time to realize and feel that:

"I'm connected to the Infinite Source! We are all connected to the Infinite Source."

"I am finally free from the idea that anyone would look down on me."

If ever you find yourself in a situation and you are among others and feel that they are looking down on you, take the time and think this thought: "הריני מקבל עלי מצות עשה של ואהבת לרעך כמוך"—I just can't help it. I'm so in love with the Jewish People that I'm stuck with this habit.

The Baal Shem Tov taught that there are three loves a person must work to perfect his whole life: loving God, loving the Torah, and loving the Jewish People.

This is what one must always know when faced with a challenge of *emunah*: Absolute *emunah* is a thought away! "I find myself to be always in a state of joy. I believe with perfect faith that the Shechinah is by my side and watches over me."[14]

Even though at this moment it appears that you are not living the dream, put yourself in that state, visualize, and feel as if you have accomplished your mission or are in the process of fulfilling your mission and say with conviction: "I'm living the dream."

---

13 *Berachos* 60b–61a.
14 Baal Shem Tov, *Tzavaas HaRivash* 137.

Always live and know that God is King—ה׳ מלך, ה׳ מלך, ה׳ ימלוך לעולם ועד! Or, as I like to say: "*Ein Sof* rules!"

"I am finally free of all material influences to pursue spiritual matters."

If you ever find yourself in a situation when you feel that you are lacking, contemplate the following: "Is there a place where the completeness of God ends and I begin?"

TOXIC THOUGHTS TO BE AVOIDED

Since we are on the subject of a kosher-thought diet, I feel that just as in the world some foods should be avoided or some substances are outright dangerous, so too, these two thoughts must be avoided at all costs:

- "My own strength and personal power brought me all this success" (*Devarim* 8:17). If you look into the Aramaic translation of the next verse, which states: "You must remember that it is God your Lord Who gives you the power to become prosperous," *Onkelos* translates it as "God put into your mind the advice of such and such a business." Bottom line, all success comes from God.

- "It's because of my righteousness that God brought me to occupy this land" (*Devarim* 9:4). The Torah is specifically referring to the Jewish People being able to drive out the wicked nations and inherit the Land of Israel. However, one should aways keep the attitude in mind that all success that comes to a person is never because of the person's righteousness, but rather it all comes from the kindness of God.[15]

---

15   *Shaarei Teshuvah* 3.

CHAPTER SEVEN
FOCUSING

If you're sincere and you know what you want, you can never fail.

Rabbi Nota Greenblatt

THE QUESTION of "What do you want?" is often answered by many with a lot of uncertainty. Many wills flow through our minds, and it might be a challenge to get a grip on one. As we mentioned the imagery in chapter one, one's thoughts could be as an airplane with an engine on one wing facing one way, and on the other wing the engine is facing the opposite direction. In other words, one will go in circles, not getting anywhere.

And suppose you can get clarity on what you want. How do you hold onto it and bring about its cultivation as a seed planted in the ground?

PERSONAL PRAYER

I have found nothing greater for the exercise of the will than prayer. My *rebbi*, Rabbi Mordechai Goldstein, would call prayer the "aerobics of the will." Why is prayer a focus of will?

One clear reason is the fact that during prayer, you must express in words what it is that you want. Your will now has an expression in words that seek manifestation, and the more you repeat that desire or will, the more focused the energy will be.

We must always remember what we spoke about earlier: that prayer is not about changing God's mind. It's about changing ourselves to become the vessel for whatever it is that we are seeking. As we pray, we are actually developing and growing the will.

A place where we see this is in the format of many prayers we make using the words:

"May there be will before You God and God of my fathers…"[1] The text does not say "May it be *Your* will" (as some do translate it as such), but rather "Let there be will" in general. I have heard in the name of the renowned Rabbanit Yemima Mizrachi that it means: "We now have the will for You, God, to fill this desire. My will has reached the level and is now the vessel for this blessing that You will bestow."

There are many wills coming from the lower part of ourselves and many coming from the higher part of our souls. This verbal meditation helps us gain clarity and bring to the forefront the good points about ourselves, e.g., our innermost holy desires, and weeds out the undesirable wills or negative thinking habits and perceptions that hold us back. This is because, along with expressing the "what" we want in prayer, we must have a clear and reasonable "why" we want that particular thing.

As we mentioned, the word for prayer in Hebrew (*pallel*) is also the root of the word "judge." What's being judged here? One explanation is that with the articulation of the person's desires, they have to look at what they are praying for and judge to see if this thing they want is justified. The person who is having a discussion with the Creator must explain why they should get it. Is it coming from the lowest aspect of their soul or the higher elements of their *neshamah*? (It's OK to have both; one just needs to focus on being truthful and sincere.)

---

1   Many have this text in the prayers we say on Rosh Hashanah when we dip the apple in the honey and other foods of symbolic nature.

The person must now dig deep into their heart for that clarity. The deeper into the person's heart it is coming from, the higher aspect of their soul they are reaching, and it becomes like the impact of an arrow shot from the bow.[2]

The greater the "why" when talking before the *Ein Sof*, the more energy and motivation will be created. Many times, when we hear our own "why" being expressed, we will see that it's not a truthful, deep, or meaningful "why" but a superficial one. For example, if I pray to God for a car or to lose weight, why do I want that new car or to lose that weight? To be like the Joneses? To look good? Or do I want it so I can have freedom to move or greater health to take care of my family or other people in a better way? Many times, it's not about the things we ask for but what those things give to us in a deeper way, such as freedom or security, etc. Really, if we can achieve greater clarity as to "why" we want it, i.e., by utilizing prayer, which digs and brings out the deep, true reason buried in the innermost part of our souls, we can overcome any obstacle.

The reshaping of the will actually transforms us into different people. Through the prayer process, we are able to distinguish our lower wills vis-a-vis our higher wills. Through this realization and distinguishing, going through the reasons why and finding the "higher why," we attach ourselves to our higher wills and become different people. We are what we think, and prayer is thinking. Hence, the higher prayer elevates us to be considered different people. Hence the Jewish custom that at the conclusion of our prayer service in a synagogue, we should exit through a different door.[3]

---

2   See *Bereishis* 48:22, where Yaakov mentions how he conquered the city of Shechem with his sword and bow. *Rashi* there interprets "sword" and "bow" as his prayer and requests, respectively. Requests are compared to the bow and arrow: The more one draws back the bowstring, the farther the arrow will travel.

3   See *Shulchan Aruch, Orach Chaim* 151:5; *Be'er Heitev* ad loc. 8; *Mishnah Berurah* ad loc. 21.

We are instructed to pray for everything—whether it be a pencil, our keys, or money for a surgical procedure. Everything that we encounter is meant to awaken us to pursue a personal relationship with God. He is the ultimate Source, and we must fully realize that there is no other source. I can only recommend that the reader delve into books about prayer to realize the great importance of this and to retrain their way of thinking.[4]

SPIRITUAL ACCOUNTING

> *Contemplate the loss of a mitzvah against its gain and the gain of a sin against its loss.*
>
> Pirkei Avos 2:1

In many of the courses I have taken, I encountered the Unified Will exercise, taught by Rabbi Aryeh Nivin, founder of Rabbi Aryeh Nivin's Chaburas and The Machon HaAdam HaShalem.[5]

When one is facing a chronic bad habit, working to develop a good habit, or perhaps dealing with the challenge of a good deed, there could be some serious resistance or even denial.

The following exercise helps one not only to reach clarity but also retrain the mind in its thinking.

The mind is said to be very much like a computer. If you ask it a question, an answer can usually be generated. The question process forces an answer and perhaps an insight to possible solutions. The challenge is to develop the right question. Using the questions brought

---

[4] See, e.g., Rabbi Nachman of Breslov, *Outpouring of the Soul*, trans. Rabbi Aryeh Kaplan.
[5] Rabbi Nivin takes Classic Torah Wisdom and translates it into practical and powerful tools to improve the wellbeing and vitality of his students and clients. Every week, he reaches hundreds of individuals throughout the world, in both his private practice and by hosting his weekly teleconference. For more information and to enlist, email breakthroughone1@gmail.com. Any material taken from his seminar is used with permission.

below triggers the mind to contemplate things that were always there yet not consciously thought of before. This is why it is recommended to go over it and over it, as we know repetition is the mother of skill. Rabbi Nivin's wonderful program incorporates and advises to do this with a loving and supporting partner in order to maximize the benefits.

One must first understand that we have within ourselves a lower soul and a higher soul.[6] Our lower soul is very childlike. It wants everything now and is very prone to the influences of the outside world and habit. It doesn't always do the right thing. The idea is to convince him to get on board with the higher will. The higher soul, of course, is only concerned with fulfilling the will of the Creator through performing the 613 mitzvos, which is its life force and completion. So, if he were to contemplate losses and gains, he could rationally convince the lower soul to do the right thing. So, a way to do that is to ask questions that force him to contemplate and arrive at a conclusion.

When asking the initial questions, we were instructed not to think too deeply but rather to feel the immediate response inside. Really "don't think," just let the answer come out. We are tapping into and opening up communication with a deeper sense of self.

When confronting a habit, such as cigarette smoking, we will ask our higher soul:

On a scale of 1 to 10, how much do you want to quit? _____

Now we ask our lower soul the same question:

On a scale of 1 to 10, how much do you want to quit? _____

Let's say that your answer are as follows: Higher soul, 9; lower soul, 2. Adding them up to 11, we then divide by two and get 5.5.

---

[6] Rabbi Chaim Vital, *Shaarei Kedushah*, chap. 1. Also, we mentioned above about the good inclination versus the evil inclination and how to convince the "old foolish king" to get on board for its own benefit.

The ideal would be to move that average to 6 or 7, or higher, at least to tip the scales. 5.5 is considered low. The gravity force of the lower soul ends up pulling the will to the lower end downward.

Then we ask the more contemplative questions, addressing the higher soul and the lower soul together. It is recommended to write down the answers, since doing so makes for a stronger impression. You can also verbally express them, but in order to maximize benefits, as I have said earlier, you will need to go over that thought for a while to affect a reprogramming.

- Higher soul, what do you gain if you quit smoking?
- What do you lose if you quit smoking?
- What do you gain if you don't quit smoking?
- What do you lose if you don't quit?

When we answer the questions with sincerity, we should discover and clarify what we gain and what we lose.

After going through the contemplation, we repeat the same questions from the beginning:

How much on a scale of 1 to 10, does your upper soul want to quit? _____

How much on a scale of 1 to 10, does your lower soul want to quit? _____

The numbers should have changed. If not, one needs to ask them all over again with sincerity to contemplate the loss versus the gain.

In repeating the process, we are retraining and reprogramming our thinking, habituating ourselves to focus on the higher soul's desires, which we achieve when we don't think too deeply but allow for the inner feeling to come out. Weighing the loss incurred versus the gain over and over and over again can retrain the mind to get an edge over the lower soul.

THE FOUR QUESTIONS MEDITATION

The Four Questions Meditation comes from my father, Dr. Harvey Cohen, who always uses this as a way to get one into a higher, more creative state.

As we mentioned, asking questions usually prompts answers. These four questions done in a contemplative fashion will also assist the will to reach a higher, elevated level of thinking.

1. Do I, ____, really believe experiences and conditions in my life are the forms of my beliefs, thoughts, and feelings to some degree?[7]
2. Do I, ____, really believe the only thing absolutely necessary for transforming any lack, limitation, fear, or concern in my life into greater peace and harmony are the appropriate contemplations, thoughts, and feelings, and nothing else?
3. Do I, ____, really believe I have the potential to think the appropriate thoughts for transforming any lack, limitation, fear, or concern in my life into greater peace and harmony?
4. Do I, ____, really understand that just by realizing, as I am now realizing, I have the potential to contemplate the appropriate thoughts for transforming any lack, limitation, fear, or concern in my life into greater peace and harmony? Am I, in fact, contemplating the appropriate thoughts?

To repeat these questions engenders one into a more creative state. Rather than being a victim of circumstances, God forbid, one should make every effort to be proactive and ignite one's creativity. It might

---

[7] Whatever the Holy One, blessed be He, throws at us, we can initiate a creative reaction—a reaction of faith and connection knowing everything God does is for the best. It could be that you are thinking or believing a certain way, and the Unlimited Creative Intelligence wants to show you that something needs changing. The change always begins in thoughts and feelings.

not change the outcome, but one's relationship to the outcome will be different, which will most likely transform a person into a more faithful being, which will in turn cause one to be a different vessel. It's certainly worth a shot!

CHAPTER EIGHT
DYNAMIC WORLD CHANGE

WE ARE TAUGHT that all Israel are guarantors of one another. The simple understanding is that we are all responsible for each other. If one person becomes elevated and does the right thing, everyone gets elevated. If, God forbid, someone degrades and commits transgressions, that person brings the entire ship down with him. The deeper idea, as we have mentioned, comes from another meaning for the Hebrew word guarantors, *areivim*, which also means "blended," the explanation being that in everyone's soul is a "sliver" of everybody else's soul.

With this comes another possible insight that can assist humanity. Since we know from the Baal Shem Tov that our thoughts are garments for our soul, it would naturally suggest that, on some level, since we are all connected with each other on a soul level, perhaps there is a possible connection we all have in the area of thoughts as well.[1]

There is a famous story of Rabbi Yosef Karo, author of the *Shulchan Aruch*, the Code of Jewish Law. He was troubled with a question on a text for many days. He prayed and worked for an answer. Finally, after many hours and days, an answer popped into his head that was sufficient, and he was very happy. After achieving his answer, he

---

1   To some degree, we are taught that one cannot know another person's thoughts (*Pesachim* 54b). However, the Baal Shem Tov and many other rabbis were able to do so on a certain level.

then went on a stroll. When he came across a synagogue where there were some businessmen learning, these businessmen happened to be studying the exact topic that the rabbi was learning, so he listened in. As he listened, he overheard one of the men ask the same question that had been bothering Rabbi Karo for many days, and then suddenly, the other person answered the exact answer that the rabbi had worked so hard to achieve. He answered it in a second! The rabbi went home astounded and broken. He found relief only afterward when he learned the principle of the wondrous bird:

Picture a village of people who are busy doing their work when, suddenly, a wondrous bird of special colors and song flies above them. Its nest was too high for anyone to reach. The king became aware of this bird and decided that he would like to have it, but no one could reach the bird. The king provided the technique that the men should form a human pyramid, allowing the person on top to reach the bird. Once he reached the nest and brought it down, the king and everyone else would be able to derive benefit from the bird.[2]

So too, in the case of the rabbi. There are tools of higher living that exist. For many people, they are just out of reach of their consciousness. It just takes a wise man, a righteous and focused man, to somehow reach up and grasp these tools of higher living. Once he grasps them, they are free for all to enjoy.[3]

---

2   *Kol Sippurei HaBaal Shem Tov*, vol. 2, p. 220; *Sippurei Chassidim*, vol. 1, p. 337. The story comes from an incident where the students were all in synagogue praying together with the Baal Shem Tov, who usually was engaged in prayers long after the others concluded. Instead of waiting for him to finish, they went home for a bite to eat, and upon returning to the synagogue, they found their *rebbi* waiting. He then told them this parable to explain that he was the one on top of the pyramid, about to bring down a novel idea. When they all left, though, he had not been able to maintain his high position to retrieve the "mystic bird."

3   The explanation of bringing down the high idea for all to benefit from I heard from my master and teacher, Rabbi Shabtai Teicher.

Our forefathers Avraham, Yitzchak, and Yaakov fixed the original "phone lines" so that we can make a "direct call" to the Creator. This is one of the reasons why we mention them in the first words of the daily silent prayer. The forefathers also brought down many other ideas of higher living being connected to the Divine, which so many of us take for granted. Moshe and all the rest of the holy rabbis also worked and sacrificed *l'shem Shamayim*, for Heaven's sake, which when achieved is of ultimate benefit to humanity and the world. They reached high into the cosmos for that simple solution or idea, and once they got it, it became available to all of us.

To expand our understanding of how we are connected, even on the thought level, I will introduce to you a study of a theory known as morphogenic fields.[4] Dr. Rupert Sheldrake, a contemporary biologist, reintroduced and developed a theory known as morphogenic fields or morphic resonance. Dr. Sheldrake was perplexed by many questions concerning certain observed phenomena of how living organisms form and come into being. Conventional science and the mechanistic model ascribe the organization of cells to the DNA—that within the DNA is encoded the structure of the entire organism. However, there still is the question of what tells the unformed homogenous cell to be a heart cell and the pre-lung cell where to go and how to act. This and other questions involving the regulation and regeneration of living organisms led Dr. Sheldrake to the concept of morphogenic fields.

These energy fields are similar in a certain way to how we experience magnetic, gravitational, or electrical fields in the world. Dr. Sheldrake proposes a type of memory in nature where the habits and behavior of any given species in the past build up and through a process he

---

[4] Michael Talbot, *Beyond the Quantum* (1986). Although it is not traditional to bring from external sources, I feel this could offer us an idea to better picture the concept of our interconnectedness.

calls "morphic resonance," which affects the habits and behavior of members of the same species—a sort of "intraspecies communication."

Dr. Sheldrake explained that thoughts and behaviors that become habitual in a sufficient number of people—whether beneficial to the human race or not—would become increasingly easier for other individuals to "tune into."

One place where this was evident was from a study by Harvard professor, Dr. William McDougall, who, over a thirty-four-year period, observed the rate of speed that rats could swim through a water-filled maze. The object was to prove genetic coding in the rats to explain how every succeeding generation would go through the "T" shaped maze faster and faster. The shock came that when they took rats from untrained genetic lines and put them into the maze, they were able to go through at the same rate of improvement as the trained set. The education or training seemed to move through the species.

Another example is the skinner pigeons that were named after the researcher, B.F. Skinner. Pigeons were brought into a box containing lighted panels: one for food, one for water, and one for heat. When he first began to do the experiments, it took a lengthy period of time to get the pigeons to even begin to peck, while later researchers found it unnecessary to work on training, because the pigeons seemed to know it right way.

This study also extends into the human species.

In October 1982, the Scientific Periodical offered a cash prize to any of their readers who could come up with an experiment that could test Sheldrake's hypothesis. One of those experiments was done with certain undiscernible pictures that would only be apparent after looking at them for a long time. In November 1984, the BBC obliged Dr. Sheldrake to show the puzzle pictures to millions of people on TV. After the solution was given, they then tested people who were never showed the puzzles, and they were able to solve it much faster.

Dr. Sheldrake claims that there are many other testable experiments that have been done that imply this interconnectedness of social groups or species beyond the brain.[5]

In sum, the idea being expressed here is that when there is critical mass of a certain species adopting an idea, it can influence the rest of the species in an "psychic" way.

The *Shem MiShmuel* speaks about how the mitzvah of sukkah protects against the thoughts of the nations. Quoting from the *Zohar*, which likens the mitzvah of sukkah to the ark of Noach, he explains that the degraded thoughts of the nations are compared to flood waters seeking to influence the minds of Israel. Even though Israel has come out victorious from judgment after Yom Kippur, they are still being pursued by the thoughts of the nations that seek to enter the holy intentions of Israel. Those external thoughts seek to influence Israel's inner motives, persuading Israel to invest their worldly blessings to indulge in the pleasures of this world instead of Israel's natural inclination to invest in pursuing Godliness. The mitzvah of sukkah offers protection against these thoughts, like the ark of Noach.[6]

From this text, we can see that there is influence in thought among the same species. I would go so far to say that since the nations are much more numerous than Israel, which makes up less than one

---

5   Other examples are studies that were done with people who felt they were being looked at from behind. Other studies of experiences include someone thinking of a certain person and suddenly that very person calls on the phone. Also, cases of nursing mothers who felt milk coming and knew their baby was waking up, even though they don't hear their baby crying. There was also an undocumented study of monkeys on various islands who were given sweet potatoes dumped on the sand. When a certain number of monkeys in one island learned to wash the potatoes to not have to spit out the sand, the monkeys on the other islands began washing their potatoes as well. Hence a good portrait of a "critical mass effect."

6   Yom Kippur, 5673. He also explains that this is why, during the festival of Sukkos, we still pray to be saved from those pursuing intentions. These are the special prayers called *Hoshanos*, which were specially instituted in the morning prayer service during these times.

percent of the world's population, those thoughts are likened to a flooding of the world, and we are caught in the middle of those "raging waters." We are so few in the world that we need the protection from the bombardment of distracting thoughts. The sukkah is the special protection from those thoughts.

This gets us to another idea more commonly known as the critical mass effect. We do see the phenomenon in the world where certain ideas or products suddenly spread like wildfire to the point that everyone needs to share the idea or purchase that item. Whatever or however the ideas spread through various means—be it good salesmen, influencers, morphic resonance, etc.—there is an influence.[7]

There was a study done on groups meditating in certain crime-filled areas of the United States. These groups would sit in an apartment and contemplate peaceful thoughts and having those peaceful thoughts extending to the local community. They found that there was a reduction of violent crimes committed in those periods.[8]

Meditation used to be a mainstream practice in Judaism. However, for some reason, it faded out some 100 to 150 years ago. One can only imagine the potential ramifications if it were to be revived again.

Other studies actually determined that our bodies influence others, outside the realm of words, vocal tone, and body postures. They call them "biophotons."

---

7   See article at https://www.nature.com/articles/s42005-022-00845-y, where it goes into various studies and results of the critical mass effect.
8   In 1960, Maharishi Mahesh Yogi predicted that one percent of a population practicing the Transcendental Meditation technique would produce measurable improvements in the quality of life for the whole population. This phenomenon was first documented in scientific research in 1976 when it was found that when 1% of a community practiced TM, the crime rate was reduced by 16% on average. At this time, the phenomenon was named the Maharishi Effect.

Back in 1974, biophysicists demonstrated the vibrational behavior of so-called junk DNA as the primary source of ultra-weak light emission, also known as biophotons. And biophotons can now be detected by the radiations emanating from our hearts and brains.

In 1926, Russian embryologist Alexander Gurvitsch discovered the emission of light from cells in a living organism. He called them mitogenic. Then, in 1974, German researcher and Nobel Prize nominee in physics, Fritz Albert Popp, reconfirmed the existence of these mitogenic rays and changed their name to biophotons. He verified that all biological systems transmit light and information, and that these subatomic light particles emit from every living system, including our body's cells and DNA.

A study conducted by German researchers at the University of Kassel shows that the chest (heart center) of an average person emits twenty biophotons per person. Yet, if a person meditates on his heart center and sends love and light to others, his heart emits an amazing 100,000 photons per second.

THE INNER AND OUTER OF CREATION

In his writings of the *Sulam*, Rabbi Yehudah Leib Ashlag gives an explanation why the Jewish People are responsible for the problems in the world. He explains that with everything in Creation, there is an inner element and an outer element. The Jewish People are considered the inner element, while the nations of the world are the outer element. Within the Jewish People, there is also an inner and an outer; the inner is those who are aligned with the Torah, which is the blueprint of Creation, while the outer is those who are not.

Even within in the inner element of those who are observant, there is an inner and an outer: those who study the Kabbalah and the innermost part of the Torah, understanding that it is the ultimate soul food, and those who only study the outermost parts of the Torah.

This is the core in which whatever happens here in this inner part has a reverberatory effect on the outer part. However the Jewish person views his soul and what it needs, since he is in this cosmic inner core, it will affect what goes on the world. If he knows and believes in his soul, and knows that the inner Torah is what needs to be emphasized, then the outer part of the world sees the soul of the world as being the vital part of its existence and pays attention to its directives and needs.

If, on the other hand, the observant Jew sees his soul as secondary to his body and puts more emphasis on his bodily desires, in essence he scorns his soul. This creates the reverberatory effect that the outside (even the non-religious Jew) will look on the observant Jew with disdain and scorn and conclude that they are not worth supporting. This, in turn, causes the nations of the world to look upon the entire Jewish nation and seek their demise.

This is why, even though the Jewish People are so few and represent so little in terms of their thoughts, they can overpower the thoughts of the nations that are so much more numerous than they are. Just as a human body is composed of different types of limbs, some are vital to the life of the body, and some limbs are not. So too, the Jewish People must know that they are likened to the vital parts of the body. We stand at the core, closest to the power Source, which of course exerts more influence.

Given all the theories we have stated above about how thoughts influence, the point here is that for us Mount Sinai people, it's worth a shot. The mission of the Jewish People is to be a light among the nations and kingdom of priests. That means to live and express Godlike attitudes and behaviors.

We have been endowed with great abilities for many things. In reality, it is our responsibility. We are descendants of the highest spiritual giants, and all of our souls were infused at Mount Sinai with this potential. The observant among us are already practicing. What we need is a little more concentrated focus to bring it to the tipping point.

The issue we face is doing the mitzvos by rote. They are habits performed with scanty awareness, and mindfulness could elevate those actions. This is why the study of the Kabbalah and Chassidic thought come into play. They deepen and give more meaning to the actions that could fall to routine.

So now, here is the challenge: To welcome yourself to the critical mass club introducing the higher idea, to accept upon yourself to be a more Godlike loving person: Godlike in thought, Godlike in speech, and Godlike in action.[9]

But how? By forming groups that would practice these principles, whether it be once a week or once a month. Even if people are not available to join in groups, then at least get a study partner who can help focus and refocus.

The program would begin with the idea we covered earlier, utilizing the "Az" concept in which we create the feeling tone of the desired situation before it actually happens—to use the power of our Godlike creative mind to feel as if we are already there and as if we have the idea already. The first step in accessing this feeling tone would be to know in truth that, in the spiritual realm, there is no time: no past, present, or future in a dimension we can only reach by means of our true, soul essence. It's beyond us to picture, but for now we can make efforts to draw from the Infinite—to put our minds and hearts as if we were in that place in the spiritual realm where all is fixed.

This could be the belief and trust that the Infinite Creator is seeking. We must reach beyond the limits in any way we can and shoot for the highest. Is it possible that God would want to hold back such

---

9   See Rabbi Moshe Cordovero, *Tomer Devorah*.

a connection and such an experience? Not for personal redemption, and certainly not for global redemption.

What would it feel like to awaken in the morning to the event that the redemption of the world is actually happening before our very eyes? Try not to put pictures or images on it but rather use these following words to engender a feeling tone: "We have finally reached the day!" Just allow ourselves to feel as if that revelation of the Infinite expression is now experienced by all of Creation in a positive way. Utilize these words: "Today is the day where I am finally free from all concerns. All barriers in my heart and mind have been fully and finally removed. I fully recognize God everywhere in my life. All humanity fully recognizes that God is all there is." We can create a feeling as if "we are going to sing about this." As a matter of fact, in a cosmic way, in the spiritual realm, since there is no time and space; we are already singing.

What does that feel like? Even if we grasped only a fragment of that feeling, allow it to grow as if turning up a volume dial. It's that feeling that we need to practice and integrate into our being. These are the angels that we create and the vessels that we form to help facilitate the actual manifestation of the redemption in this world.

The second idea to practice would be to utilize the first thought of the day, which really should be focused on just before you go to sleep. Imagine waking up to this thought: "Today is a good day for the redemption of the world."

As I stated earlier, considering the situation on the world's current state, these thoughts should certainly be worth some effort, even the size of the eye of a needle.

ANCHORING THROUGH MELODY AND PRAYER

Anchors are stimuli that bring out thoughts and feelings. We can experience them all the time. Hearing an old song can bring us to certain feelings we had in childhood. Certain smells of certain foods give rise to certain memories. We can utilize this psychological principle in a positive way—to attach a dynamic, uplifting thought, feeling, or lesson to an action or set of words.

One way of anchoring is to play or hum a particular melody. No words, just melody. Melodies have very powerful spiritual properties.[10] They can bring the soul to a very high place. Find your favorite, powerful, uplifting melody. Play it or sing it. While you are singing it, let the words of redemption I mentioned above bring about that certain, positive feeling. You are now taking a feeling and anchoring it to a melody. This takes practice, but I find it to be extremely enlightening. I use this when I go to synagogue where they sing the songs of the late Rabbi Shlomo Carlebach, which I have found to bring me to the next level. So, because of that, whenever I hear that particular melody, no matter where I am, I will experience those happy feelings of love and connection—feelings of world redemption.

Another form of anchoring is in words. We can build up within ourselves a certain feeling, and then when we say certain words or phrases, those words then become an anchor to the feeling. This takes practice, since we are involved in training or conditioning ourselves to feel a certain way, but with enough repetition, it becomes second nature.

I find that using many lines and verses in the daily prayer book as an anchor establishes and magnifies certain feelings. In truth, prayer is called "service of the heart," which means **you have to feel it**. The words of the prayer book are not meant to be read by rote, God forbid, but rather are meant to instill an emotional charge.

---

10   The Maggid of Mezeritch, in the name of the Baal Shem Tov, said: "Using melody is one of the ways of Godly service of the Chassidim"; *Sichos* 702, p. 122. "Melody touches the soul," *Igros Hakodesh* 3:750.

Let's try this exercise:

Try going into your past and finding a time when you felt loved by someone. Any time, from anywhere. Focus on the feeling of what it felt like to be loved. Try even turning up the dial to maximum energy feeling. When you have that feeling, go to the blessing we say just before *k'rias Shema* that reads: "With abundant love You have loved us, God."[11] Right now, allow yourself to feel the feeling of love from God.

Another exercise:

Search through your memory to a time or situation when you felt an incredible feeling of love for something or someone. If that's too difficult, then make believe, to the best of your ability, a feeling of incredible love. It could be the love of a pet, love of a child, spouse, grandparent, etc. Then, once you have reached that feeling, elevate it and declare your commitment to God by saying "*Shema Yisrael*…and you shall the love the Lord, your God, with all your heart, soul, and might."[12] When practiced enough, attaching or anchoring that feeling to the verses will become automatic the next time you say those words. Once again, *tefillah* is about establishing and building those feelings.

I heard from Rabbi Shlomo Riskin himself that if a person were to be stuck on a deserted island and could only take two books with them, what should those books be? He answered: the daily prayer book and the code of Jewish law. The code of Jewish law is because you have to know what to do in the various situations, and the Jewish prayer book because most of the essential principles of Judaism are contained within its words.

Much of the daily prayer book we have today dates as far back as the Anshei K'nesses Hagedolah, including the last of the prophets

---

11   ArtScroll siddur, p. 89. The Arizal text reads "with eternal love."
12   ArtScroll siddur, pp. 90–93. Because, in truth, God is the Source of all love, and all your feelings of love need to be elevated to the Source.

led by Ezra (480–440 BCE).[13] The special and very deep intentions of what they had in mind when compiling these prayers expands to an extensive number of books. They go from explaining the simple meaning to very deep Kabbalistic intentions.

To give you an example, the Arizal describes how through the various stages of the prayer service, one actually ascends and descends from the higher worlds. For example, through the blessings of the morning to the section of the praises, one's soul moves from the level of the world of *Asiyah*/Making, the lowest level of consciousness, to the world or dimension of *Yetzirah*/Formation, i.e., the realm of the angels. One moves upward through *Beriah*/Creating, culminating in the silent prayer known as the *Amidah*, or *Shemoneh Esreh*, the eighteen blessings, where the person praying reaches the highest realm of the world of *Atzilus*/Nearness.

The general idea of prayer, as we have mentioned, is that we don't change God's mind but rather we change ourselves and become a completely different person.[14] I have no intention of deviating from the classic understanding of any of the intentions, be they simple or Kabbalistic. My only intention is to merely make use of the words we are already saying and attempting to instill a feeling tone that puts us into a more elevated state. To create angels with wings is to put awe, love, and joy in the words.

A CELEBRATION OF SOURCE

Prayer is comprised of different parts: praises, thanksgivings, and requests. This structure is already built into the daily *tefillah* experience.

---

13   *Berachos* 33a; *Megillah* 17b; *Rambam, Mishneh Torah, Tefillah* 1:4.
14   *Orach Chaim* 151:5; see *Mishnah Berurah* ad loc., 21, and *Be'er Heitev* ad loc. 8, that when one leaves the synagogue, he should exit from a different door in order to demonstrate to himself that he is not the same person.

- Praises—because we must fully realize before Whom we are standing to have an increased awareness of the Unlimited Source.
- Thanksgivings—because we must always begin with appreciating what we have. Gratitude is the key to our redemption, as it forms us into being that vessel to receive more and embeds in our awareness not to take things for granted.
- Requests—because we have a special relationship with the Creator to participate and partner in the completion of Creation.

In a more general way, I like to look at *tefillah* in general as a celebration of the Source. I say this because I consider the thought:

"Is it possible that God would withhold His absolute goodness from us? From me?"

What would it be like to fully embody the above statement?[15] Hold onto it for a bit. Try to put all your suffering, lacking, and questions aside and permit yourself to feel this overwhelming attitude from the Infinite Source.

Our *emunah* demands that we know that God is the only Source of everything.

So, I look at prayer not so much as coming to the Creator with a "give me" list, but rather as a type of experience of knowing He is the Source and also joyously celebrating that it will be given.

BARUCH ATAH HASHEM—THE MINTED COIN OF BLESSING

This function of thinking has already been built into our daily *tefillah* service.

---

15 If you answered yes to this question, then I would recommend re-contemplating your relationship with the Infinite. Could it be that perhaps because in some way you're thinking the opposite? That God does withhold? Could it be that the very thought of such an attitude—that He would withhold—participates in your experience of lack? Of course, there is suffering in our lives and the world, but perhaps it's worth asking the question, since your thoughts create angels.

All blessings begin with the same first words: "Blessed are You, Hashem, our Lord, King of the universe." The nickname for those first words is termed "the minted coin" of the blessing. It's a stamp the Sages placed that all blessing should begin with. As the Sages have written them, blessings are always a way for us to focus and realize that there is a Source from which this unique experience is coming from— from food to the function of your body upon leaving the restroom, and many more.

Even in the time before I was a mitzvah-practicing Jew, I felt that there should be a declaration over a fruit to acknowledge that there is a Creator. When I arrived at the yeshiva where they taught me blessings to say over all manners of things, my joy was boundless.

The blessings that we say begin with the word, "*Baruch*," which is loosely translated as "blessed." This word needs to be understood more deeply in our attempt to connect with God. The holy masters write that the word really means "more of" and "increase."[16] Another early master writes that its meaning is "source," or "pool where the source is."[17] How do we put these two meanings together?

Picture being a guest in someone's house, and they offer you a piece of freshly baked pie. You take a taste, and it's wonderful. Upon finishing the small taste, you ask for more. I look at it as two sides of the same coin: On one side is acknowledgment of the source of where this wonderful pie is coming from, and the other side is a request for more.

The same thing is at play with blessings; there is a double function. "God, I acknowledge that You are the Source and I want more. A hidden idea is the fact that you have already tasted the experience. Otherwise, how could you be expressing the desire for more? So, you envision in a blessing that you have already been answered to some degree and

---

16 Rabbi Chaim Volozhin, *Nefesh Hachaim*, shaar 2.
17 Rabbi Yosef Gikatilla, *Shaarei Orah*, chap. 1.

only wish for the increase. With this idea, the word "*baruch*" takes on a whole different experience—an actual drawing down of an influx of experience.

Much is to be said about this drawing down of influx that the Kabbalists have written about, whether it be a spiritual or physical influx. Whatever it is, we take part in drawing it down.

Now, this is our daily challenge: To actually contemplate these ideas when making a blessing and saying the word "*baruch*." Whether we make a blessing on food or give praise upon leaving the restroom, we have to focus our mind on what is actually being expressed by the word "*baruch*": "Source are You, more of You, God, Who creates the fruit of the tree." In a sense, we are saying: "May Your Presence increase now; May You be more recognized in the world, that You are the Source."

The next word of a blessing is the word "You." It is not very common in other cultures to refer to a dignitary or someone of honor as "you." When addressing someone of high status, many other cultures refer to such a person in the third person, for example, "Would the Rabbi like a cup of tea?" Yet, we, who are so intimate with the Unlimited, can actually address Him with the word "You." Hence, this word should produce a feeling of great intimacy.

The next word is the name of God. All names are revelations. Any name is a concept, and we know that the Unlimited Creator is beyond concept. We need names as a "handle," so to speak, a vessel to at least grasp some concept. The law of what to contemplate when saying the Tetragrammaton is written in the law books. There is one pronunciation and two contemplations:

א-ד-נ-י—Master over everything; and י-ה-ו-ה—The "IS."

The classic intention and meditation for this name is really "was, is, and will be." This is because the letters spell out in Hebrew those three words: "היה הווה ויהיה," as the classic commentators explain. This is because we are coming from the finite dimension of time. This is how we "get a grip." Although the letters of this name do spell out the words for past, present, and future, a more appropriate contemplation would be "constantly present" or "Eternal IS."[18]

This covers the first three words of all blessings. So, when we say those first three words over a piece of fruit, for example, we say *"Baruch Atah Hashem* [Blessed are You, God], Who created the fruit of the tree," we can contemplate: "Increase now, Infinite Source, Who created the fruit of the tree."

Rabbi Avraham Yitzchak Kook gives us an amazing insight into prayer in general. He says that, in truth, our innermost soul is always praying 24/7, and when we approach prayer, we are stepping into that higher part of ourselves. He poetically describes the praying soul as a blossoming rose that opens to greet the dew and sunlight from where its life comes: Acknowledging, appreciating, and enhancing the experience of the Infinite Source.

THE SILENT PRAYER MEDITATION

Many of the blessings are written in the present tense. Why? Because according to the formula of *emunah* that we have been discussing, we must envision the prayer *as if* we already are in the process of being answered and receiving it.

The silent, standing prayer service, which should be looked at as a meditation, can be a major exercise in practicing your bringing into awareness and allowing the Source to be manifest in Creation in the way of whatever we are praying for—whether it be personal redemption, healing the sick, or bringing livelihood. To feel the feeling as if God is giving it to you and you only wish for more—not only for yourself, but also for the entire world.

---

18 See *Leshem Shevo V'Achlamah, Sefer Hakdamos*, chap. 2.

I find that when we are in this state of ultimate connection with the Creator, there is a window or doorway that is opened. If we have an issue in our lives or a difficult challenge in our Torah studies, answers or insights pop in. I find this especially true during the prayers we say on Shabbos. Many times, a window into my potential and the potential of the world as a whole are pictured. It is indeed bringing down the bird of wonder!

With the power of our minds, hearts, and faith, we have the potential to draw the reality of whatever blessing or prayer we are saying into our experience as if it is happening now. "Source, You are Unlimited, Who heals all flesh, Who blesses the years, Who gathers the exiles, Who builds Jerusalem, Who blesses Israel with peace."

I believe that as we gather in the synagogues, we constantly exercise our faith and put ourselves in the quantum realm beyond time and space of the reality of whatever blessing we are praying for. We are visualizing and actualizing with our whole being that God is bringing about that reality at that moment. Could this possibly be an intention of the Men of the Great Assembly who wrote the prayer book—the beginning of each of the blessings as a recognition of lack and therefore taking the form of a request, but the end of each of those eighteen blessings being the manifestation? Based on knowing our dynamic creative potential, wouldn't you say it's worth a shot? I'm not saying we shouldn't be begging and pleading for God's compassion, but we should also always come with the attitude that He has that compassion and that it's certainly coming.

Now, since we are instructed to do this three times a day, imagine if everyone who was praying would adopt this way of praying? I would think that our critical mass, which already has an effect, would have an even greater effect.

In a deeper sense, these prayers were written in such a way and meant to be said in a group to maximize the energy. Groups always have the potential to increase the energy, hence the idea of going to a synagogue to pray would of course enhance the experience and the effect. This can work in any synagogue, and especially if you can find a synagogue that utilizes inspiring melodies.

MICRO-MAN, MACRO-MAN

The book of the *Zohar* reiterates the concepts of micro and macro. The text reads, "Man is a small world."[19] This means that man includes all things. At the beginning of man's creation, when God said, "Let us make man," all the commentators ask: With whom is God speaking? There are many answers, but I will bring the explanation of the Arizal. He explains that as God diminished His light in order that Creation not be overwhelmed by the Infinite light, many worlds were created. These worlds serve as filters in a way to diminish that light. The world or dimension closest to the Infinite light is called *Atzilus*, which translates as "nearness." The next level down is called *Beriyah*/Creation, then *Yetzirah*/Formation, and last *Asiyah*/Making, which is our realm.

All of Creation is contained in these realms. When God said "let us make man," He was asking each one of these realms to invest and contribute of themselves for the creation of man. Therefore, contained within man is a spiritual element of everything, including the "portion of God on High."[20] This put man in a powerful situation in which we are an interconnected cosmic web, where our seemingly small actions have very powerful effects. If man messes up, all the realms suffer, because it blocks the light and blessing from coming into all those worlds. If he succeeds, all the universes are blessed and receive their necessary sustenance.

---

19 *Tikkunei Zohar* 130b.
20 *Sefer Baal Shem Tov, Parashas Va'eschanan* #13; *Sefer Tanya*.

One must always look at the world as if it is poised on the scale between merit and obligation. Do one mitzvah, and you tip the scales to the side of merit. Do one transgression, and you tip the scale to the side of obligation.[21] This can be overwhelming, but I am only bringing this idea to negate the belief that someone might say, "What effect can my thoughts, words, or actions do?" Everything has a cosmic effect.

We are all in the process of becoming the vessel, and mankind, as a whole, is in the process as well.

If we all can realize that the thoughts we think are so powerful and have so much effect, we can know that we can effect global change, especially when we join together. Just the idea alone of this thought is already enough to effect that change—to joyously celebrate our connection to the Infinite and have a level of simple faith that He is running the show. Realize and feel that in the supernal cosmic realm, we already are that vessel. That thought itself, when realized by a critical mass, should tip the scales and introduce the world to a higher level of meaningful living.

You might ask, "Why hasn't it happened until now?" In truth, I do not know. But I do know that we are certainly closer to the redemption than ever before. As the Sage Hillel would often say, "If not now, when?" What if all we had to do was fully believe it?

WELCOMING RESISTANCE

Among the biggest resistances to these principles that I have found so far is the mirror principle mentioned in chapter three. Everybody will hear it, and many will resist it. They are just not ready to take responsibility. I feel it's like when Magellan's expedition came back

---

21   *Kiddushin* 40b: Rabbi Elazar in the name of Rabbi Shimon says that since the world is judged after the majority, and the individual is judged after the majority, if you do one mitzvah, fortunate are you that you have tipped the scales to the balance of merit.

and told everyone that the world is round, and no one listened. How long did it take until the idea was widely accepted? These, and many more such new ideas, are met with resistance. It's amazing that even though a person can logically agree to the principle, the lower soul just can't take it.

This is why it is necessary to form groups, or at least have a study partner, to review and integrate these principles into our daily lives.

If we would have enough people who utilize these thought principles through study partners or groups, we would stop blaming others, start working on ourselves, and really start lifting ourselves out of our old beliefs.

At the root of lifting ourselves out of our old belief patterns lies the need to believe in ourselves—to realize with great conviction that we are made in the image and likeness of God, to grasp that we are creating every moment, whether we believe it or not. Through our old patterns of belief, our evil inclination constantly works to convince us otherwise—that we are powerless victims of circumstances. To overcome the challenge of not believing in ourselves is to know that God believes in us. This should be at the forefront of our thinking, and this is where the idea of a study partner or support group can be vital.

This and many other ingrained beliefs will always arise to block or sabotage our personal and global development. The attitude should be to not only recognize the resistance but actually welcome it. It's all part of our development and eventually we'll reach the stage that, whenever we encounter resistance, we'll say, "Thank You, God, for bringing me this area of resistance and the opportunity to work my way through it."

EPILOGUE

I BEGAN THIS BOOK stating that I was writing it with great trepidation. I was tested, and I am still being tested, living with a broken heart over the loss of my son Elisha Meir, who passed away from brain cancer in 2014. I could easily say about myself that I didn't have enough faith, but where would that take me? To an abyss of sadness and depression. For sure, I know that this is not what the Almighty wants, and it doesn't reflect how Elisha would want me to live. He is living in the world where all can be seen clearly. Every detail of everyone's life—all the ups and downs—is absolutely necessary, no doubt about it. The highest elevation I could give to the soul of my son would be to live a life of faith and joy. So, this is what I choose to do.

APPENDIX

WE HAVE ALREADY mentioned in chapter one the phrase, "In the way in which a person wants to go, they lead him." We will now present the entire source for this statement to deepen our understanding.

Rabbah bar Rav Huna said in the name of Rav Huna; some say it was Rav Huna who said it in the name of Rabbi Elazar: It is repeated from three sources, from the Torah, from the Prophets, and from the Writings, that

"In the way that a man wants to go, they lead him."[1]

FROM THE TORAH

The first source is brought from *Sefer Bamidbar* in the narrative about the wicked prophet Bilam.

"Do not go with them…Get up, go with them."[2]

The verses here refer to the narrative of the wicked prophet Bilam, who was being asked by the Midianite king, Balak, to come and curse the children of Israel. King Balak sent emissaries to Bilam asking him to come and curse.

Bilam replied, "Stay here the night, and I will ask the Almighty."

That night, God came to him in a dream and said, "Who are these men with you?"

---

1   *Makkos* 10b.
2   *Bamidbar* 22:12, 20.

Bilam said to God, "Balak ben Tzippor, King of Moab, sent to me, saying, 'Behold, the people coming out of Egypt has covered the surface of the earth. Now go and curse it for me; perhaps I will be able to make war against it and drive it away.'"

God said to Bilam, "**Do not go with them!** You shall not curse the people, for it is blessed!"

When King Balak heard that Bilam refused to come, he again sent officers even more important than the previous ones, imploring Bilam to come curse the people.

Once again, Bilam told them to remain the night, and he would hear what God would have to say.

This time, God said to Bilam, "If the men came to summon you, **get up, go with them**, but only the thing that I speak to you—that you shall do."

It seems that God is wishy-washy! Yet, we have been taught, "I am God. I do not change."

Hence, the Talmud deduces, "The way that a man wants to go, they lead him."[3] Bilam's evil will and consciousness to go with them brought about God sending him an angel according to his will and consciousness that said to him, "get up and go with them." That's why at first God said, "Don't go," and subsequently there was a message to "get up and go."[4]

The narrative continues with other warnings from Heaven, resulting in Bilam's donkey speaking to him to knock him out of his obsession. The angel of Bilam's will to curse was too powerful and pushed him to move ahead and make three attempts to curse the Jewish People.

---

3   The following is a quasi-translation and explanation of the eighteenth-century commentator, the *Maharsha*.

4   From here, it seems the universe always says yes to some degree, so watch out what you ask for!

As we know, all his attempts failed. God put the words of blessing in Bilam's mouth, and not a curse was uttered.

If it was not for God's interference, Bilam would have succeeded. The special circumstance for God's interfering was for the sake of Israel—to show that while the Jewish People were eating their *mahn* for breakfast, oblivious to what's happening around them, God was looking out for them. That's the understanding: Telling us the message that God is looking out for us in ways beyond our knowing.

FROM THE PROPHETS

כֹּה אָמַר ה' גֹּאֲלֶךָ קְדוֹשׁ יִשְׂרָאֵל. אֲנִי ה' אֱלֹקֶיךָ מְלַמֶּדְךָ לְהוֹעִיל מַדְרִיכְךָ בְּדֶרֶךְ תֵּלֵךְ.

> Thus says God, your Redeemer, the Holy One of Israel: "I am God your Lord, Who disciplines you for your benefit, guiding you in the way you go."[5]

As with so many verses in the Torah, one must ask concerning the double language. Why does the verse need to state, "Who disciplines you for your benefit" and then "guiding you in the way you go"? The verse, "I am God, your Lord, I teach you for your benefit," tells us about the mitzvos. That since all the mitzvos are only taught to help and benefit man, hence "for your benefit." However, the next part of the verse, "guiding you," is speaking of an angel that, according to your knowing and will, guides you in that particular way. Good luck with all that, because if it's not aligned with God's will, there will be pitfalls and dangers. But as the beginning of the verse says, "thus says God your redeemer..." In the end, the Almighty will get us to our destination,

---

5   *Yeshayahu* 48:17.

despite any angels that we have been involved with creating that bring us out of that alignment.

FROM THE WRITINGS

אִם לַלֵּצִים הוּא יָלִיץ וְלַעֲנָוִים יִתֶּן חֵן.

As to the scorners, He will put them to scorn, but to the humble, He will grant grace.[6]

The verse that reads, "With the scorners, He will put them to scorn…" means to say that with the person's scoffing, He will add "the scoffer," which is the angel according to the person's scoffing. And if he will be lowly, then he will give grace to himself. God will send His corresponding angel of grace.

The question is why are there three sources or proofs? Isn't it enough with just one? One simple answer could be to bring stronger emphasis on the rule of our thoughts. Another possible explanation could be that the first source clearly tells us the principle of will and thought, the second refers to action, and the third source references words. Thus, we have the different angels of thought, action, and word.

---

6   Mishlei 3:34.

ABOUT THE AUTHOR

RABBI YAAKOV COHEN was born and raised in California. He attended Cal State University, Northridge, where he studied philosophy and psychology. He went on to study at a number of leading yeshivos in Yerushalayim where he received his Rabbinic ordination.

Rabbi Cohen has been involved in outreach in Texas for the past twenty years and continues to give classes online for TORCH of Houston. He learned Kabbalah under one of the great Kabbalists of Yerushalayim, his late father-in-law, Rabbi Shabtai Teicher. Rabbi Cohen has taught seminars and lectures on Kabbalah, mysticism, and Chassidic thought in both America and Israel, and he currently resides with his family in Ramat Beit Shemesh, Israel.

Special thanks to

MELISSA SHEPPS

May you continue to grow
in the ways of Torah and *emunah*.

In honor of
ELIAS CHEREM—ELIAHU BEN DAVID
VICTORIA BAT DIOYA
ELIAS AMKIE HACOHEN—
ELIAHU BEN AVRAHAM HACOHEN
LIDIA—LEAH BAT MALKA

May their memory be for a blessing.

DR. LAZARO CHEREM

In honor of
ELEANOR SUE BELDON KOMET

DAVID KOMET

May the *neshamos* of our grandparents have an *aliyah*

YEHUDIS BAS BINYOMIN
YITZCHAK BEN HIRSCHL
YAAKOV BEN ELCHANAN LEIB
TZERNA BAS MOSHE
YEHUDA LEIB BEN BOAZ
SIMA BAS SHMUEL

DAN GOLDFINE

In memory of

CHAYA BAT DANIEL
HERIETTE PICKEL

DANIEL AND DIKLA PICKELNER

In honor of my dear wife

JUDITH ROSENSTOCK

AND OUR CHILDREN

Jon and Amara Biro, Aaron Rosenstock, Ben and Amy Leipzig,
Deborah Leipzig, Marc and Sarah Rosenstock

AND GRANDCHILDREN

Harrison Biro, Madeline Biro, Alex Biro, Jake Leipzig,
Hannah Rosenstock, Lily Rosenstock, and Charlotte Rosenstock

DR. HARVEY ROSENSTOCK

In honor of my father
ARNOLD L. WIDEN

BRENT WIDEN

In honor of my father
VELVEL KOGAN

ELEANORA KOGAN

With thanks to
HAVIV NISAN
DAN AND ELISHEVA KULLMAN
NACHUM AND ALI FOOTNICK
DAVID MARNEL
AVRAHAM AND NECHAMA BITTING
DR. ALAN AND JANET WINTERS
ELENI M SAATSOGLOU
KATHLEEN BECK DUFFY
ALLYSON JUNE AXELROD JONES
OURIEL DZIKOWSKI